SR-71 Blackbird

Lockheed's Ultimate Spy Plane

DAVID DOYLE

SCHIFFER MILITARY

4880 Lower Valley Road Atglen, PA 19310

Designed by Justin Watkinson
Type set in Impact/Minion Pro/Univers LT Std

ISBN: 978-0-7643-6708-3
Printed in India

Published by Schiffer Publishing, Ltd.
4880 Lower Valley Road
Atglen, PA 19310
Phone: (610) 593-1777; Fax: (610) 593-2002
Email: Info@schifferbooks.com
Web: www.schifferbooks.com

For our complete selection of fine books on this and related subjects, please visit our website at www.schifferbooks.com. You may also write for a free catalog.

Schiffer Publishing's titles are available at special discounts for bulk purchases for sales promotions or premiums. Special editions, including personalized covers, corporate imprints, and excerpts, can be created in large quantities for special needs. For more information, contact the publisher.

We are always looking for people to write books on new and related subjects. If you have an idea for a book, please contact us at proposals@schifferbooks.com.

Acknowledgments

This book would not have been possible without the generous help of many friends, including Tom Kailbourn, Scott Taylor, Dana Bell, David Dwight Jackson, Tracy White, Stan Piet, Brett Stolle at the National Museum of the United States Air Force, the staff of the National Archives, and Tony Landis. Most of all, the Lord has blessed me with a wonderful wife, Denise, who not only has provided material contributions in aiding with research but has gifted me with her unflagging support, for which I am especially appreciative.

Any photos not otherwise credited are from the collection of the National Museum of the United States Air Force.

Contents

Introduction

In the late 1950s, the world's premier reconnaissance aircraft was the high-flying Lockheed U-2, such as this U-2A, serial number 56-6718. *National Museum of the United States Air Force*

An axiom found on the walls of many automotive speed shops reads something like this:

We offer three types of products:

Good–Fast–Cheap

You can pick any two

Good and Cheap won't be Fast

Fast and Cheap won't be Good

Good and Fast won't be Cheap

Lockheed could have hung this same axiom on the wall of the Skunk Works, and the SR-71 (along with its stablemates, the A-12 and YF-12) certainly represents the pinnacle of the third option.

Today, more than sixty years after the first flight of an aircraft of this series, multiple flight records set by the series still stand. Although in the latter years of their service, many of their systems, analog as they were, seemed antiquated, the aircraft still performed "as advertised." While some detractors argued that satellite reconnaissance had rendered these aircraft—known as the Blackbird or, by the men who operated them, as "the Sled" or "Habu"—obsolete, the unarguable counterpoint of this was that Blackbird could be over anywhere, at any time, without regard to orbit times or any of the other limitations of satellite surveillance. This unpredictability made concealment by the enemy much more difficult.

Indeed, it was not advancing technologies or obsolescence of the Blackbird that brought about the retirement of the finest reconnaissance aircraft the world has known—rather, it was the last line of that axiom: flying the Blackbird was not cheap. Military strategists decided that the aircraft, with their supporting equipment, were simply too expensive to operate.

On May 1, 1960, this U-2A aircraft, serial number 56-6693 (also referred to as Article 360), flown by CIA pilot Francis Gary Powers, was shot down over the Soviet Union. The force of the shoot-down ejected Powers from the plane before he could arm the destruct features of the aircraft. *Dwight D. Eisenhower Presidential Library*

Powers was ultimately exchanged for the KGB spy, Colonel William Fisher, known as Rudolf Abel, on February 10, 1962. While initially the US press was highly critical of Powers, questioning his loyalty, CIA director Allen Dulles said, "He performed his duty in a very dangerous mission and he performed it well, and I think I know more about that than some of his detractors and critics know, and I am glad to say that to him tonight." In 1998, it was revealed that Powers's mission was a joint CIA/USAF operation; thus Powers was posthumously presented the Prisoner of War Medal, as well as the CIA Director's Medal "for extreme fidelity and extraordinary courage in the line of duty." Upon his return to the US, Powers went to work for Lockheed and is seen here with Kelly Johnson, designer of the U-2, A-12, and SR-71. *National Museum of the United States Air Force*

The Soviets stayed mum about the shoot-down for a period, allowing the US government to spin a prearranged cover story that this was a weather aircraft. CIA analysts believed that the pilot could not have survived a shoot-down. To the embarrassment of the United States and President Eisenhower, this subterfuge was exposed with the display of this debris of the U-2A and the revelation that Powers had been captured alive. *National Archives*

CHAPTER 1

Oxcart: The A-12

Lockheed built special semitrailers to move the secret yet oversized A-12 from the Burbank plant to Groom Dry Lake for flight testing. Both trailers were collapsible, allowing the empty return trip to be less daunting. The bulk of the aircraft was contained in the larger trailer, while the smaller one transported the outer wing sections, rudders, and forward fuselage. The trailers were used for the duration of the Blackbird program, hauling A-12, YF-12A, and SR-71 airframes to Groom Lake and Palmdale.

Following the loss of U-2 and pilot Francis Gary Powers over the Soviet Union in May 1960, the CIA, which ran the U-2 program, sought a follow-up aircraft with lower radar cross section. The CIA code-named the project "Oxcart," but Lockheed, which had designed the U-2, known internally as the "Angel" program, fittingly gave the successor project the name "Archangel." The first proposal for the new project, designed by a team led by Clarence "Kelly" Johnson, was thus the A-1, followed by the A-2, and so on.

While the A-11 showed considerable promise, it was further refined by borrowing ideas from the competing Convair "Kingfish" proposal, the resulting improved design being the A-12. This design met the CIA requirements for low radar cross section, cruising altitude of 80,000 to 100,000 feet, and a top speed between Mach 3 and 4.

On August 29, 1959, the Lockheed design was selected, against the rival Convair offering, and on September 4 the CIA issued the company a $4.5 million advanced feasibility contract. This was followed on January 26, 1960, with the agency placing an order for twelve of the Oxcart aircraft.

Even as the project was moving forward, some had misgivings, including some in the very highest places. On June 2, 1960, Gen. Andrew Goodpaster, military aide to President Eisenhower, wrote this Top-Secret memo:

I spoke to the President early this week about the question of whether work should go forward on the successor to the U-2. After considering the matter, he said he was inclined to think it should go forward on a low priority, as a high-performance reconnaissance plane for the Air Force in the time of war. I suggested that it might be useful for Mr. Allen Dulles, Mr. (Thomas) Gates and Mr. (Maurice) Stans to get together to consider the matter, and he agreed. He said he did not think the project should be pushed at top priority. In fact, they come to the conclusion that it be best to get out of it if we could. Alternately, they may feel that we have too much invested in it that we should capitalize on this through carrying it forward.

Three A-12s are assembled at the Lockheed factory in Burbank, California, sometime between 1962 and 1964. As one of Lockheed's counterintelligence deception measures, the original caption identified these as A-11s.

To achieve the CIA goals, virtually every system in the aircraft had to be designed from scratch, often using previously untried techniques and materials. Not only that, it all had to be done in total secrecy. The airframe was made primarily of titanium to resist the 600-degree-plus temperatures produced by the friction of the air moving over the skin at high Mach numbers. Not only was little then known about forming and machining this metal, but it was also difficult to obtain—the CIA incredibly covertly purchasing the material from Soviet mines. Even the fuel was specially formulated, it too having to be heat resistant.

To power the A-12, and the subsequent Blackbird aircraft, Lockheed chose a pair of Pratt & Whitney J58 engines. The engine evolved over time, ultimately to a configuration that developed 34,000 pounds of thrust, or 160,000 shaft horsepower (shp). With two such engines, the Blackbird developed more horsepower than a battleship.

The first A-12 lifted off from Groom Lake (Area 51) on April 25, 1962, with Lockheed test pilot Lou Schalk at the controls. The aircraft, in a partially disassembled state, had been trucked from Lockheed's Burbank facility in February. As additional aircraft were completed, they too were trucked to Area 51. On May 24, 1963, the third A-12 built was lost during a subsonic test flight. Pilot Ken Collins was able to eject safely. The crash was later attributed to icing of the pitot tube. Three and a half years later, the type was declared operational. On May 31, 1967, the A-12 began to be used over Vietnam, operating from Kadena Air Force Base, Okinawa, as part of a secret operation known as Black Shield. On January 26, 1968, the A-12 flow over Korea as well, in search of the seized USS *Pueblo*, which was found by pilot Jack Weeks.

Despite the successful flights over Vietnam, and locating *Pueblo*, on May 8, 1968, the A-12 flew its final operational mission. Kelly Johnson wrote in that month that "the decision was taken to phase out the A-12 by about mid-June. Plans were put into effect for storing the A-12 aircraft at Palmdale, CA." This decision was finalized by President Johnson on May 21. June 8 was determined to be the date that the A-12s at Kadena would begin to be redeployed stateside. In the days leading up to that, on June 4, Jack Weeks took A-12 "Article 129" for a "functional checkout flight" (FCF) following an engine change but disappeared 520 miles east of the Philippines. Sensors on board the A-12 had reported to ground stations that the starboard engine exhaust gas temperature was excessive (over 1,580 degrees), while fuel flow to that engine was low, less than 7,500 pounds per hour, and the aircraft had dropped below 68,500 feet. Radio contact with Weeks was unsuccessful. An intensive search failed to turn up Weeks or any debris from the aircraft, leading most to believe it broke up in flight.

On June 21, 1968, Article 131, the aircraft that had flown the first A-12 mission over Vietnam, made the last flight of any A-12, with Ken Collins landing the aircraft in Palmdale, California, where it would be placed into storage at Plant 42.

The day of the A-12 was over; she had been upstaged by her younger sister, the SR-71.

During one of its test flights, the first A-12, manufacturer's number 121 (also referred to as Article 121) and USAF serial number 60-6924, performs a fuel dump, to lighten the aircraft preparatory to landing. This plane made its maiden flight on April 25, 1962, from Groom Lake, with test pilot Lou Schalk flying the aircraft at an altitude of 20 feet for approximately a mile and a half. The following day, Schalk flew the plane on its first full test flight. *Tony Landis collection*

The outer wings of the second A-12 built, serial number 60-6925, are raised in the Lockheed Burbank plant. Raising the wings permitted access to the Pratt & Whitney J58 engine housed in each wing.

The thirteenth and final A-12, serial number 60-6939, nears completion at Lockheed's "Skunk Works." Delivered in early 1964, the aircraft would have a short life, being lost in a landing accident on July 9, 1964, at the end of its tenth flight, having logged only 8.19 flight hours.

This A-12 is being used for engine run-up tests in March 1962. Surplus external fuel tanks are mounted atop the wings to combat fuel leakage issues during these tests. The aircraft did not fly with these tanks in place. *Lockheed via Tony Landis*

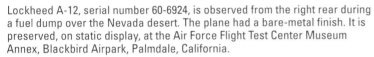

Lockheed A-12, serial number 60-6924, is observed from the right rear during a fuel dump over the Nevada desert. The plane had a bare-metal finish. It is preserved, on static display, at the Air Force Flight Test Center Museum Annex, Blackbird Airpark, Palmdale, California.

The second A-12 refuels from a KC-135Q, an aerial refueler specially equipped to handle JP-7 fuel, which was unique to the Blackbird program. This A-12 spent its entire life of 161 flights, totaling 177.52 flight hours, serving as a flight test aircraft. *Tony Landis collection*

The third A-12, serial number 60-6926, was ill fated. During a test flight on May 24, 1963, with CIA pilot Ken Collins at the controls, the plane suddenly went out of control and entered an inverted spin. Collins ejected safely, and the A-12 crashed near Wendover, Utah. An investigation discovered that the pitot tube had become iced, causing the stability augmentation system to pitch the nose upward and stall the plane, sending it into a spin from which the pilot could not recover. *Tony Landis collection*

When the CIA, which operated the A-12, began releasing information about the aircraft, this was one of the first images shown to the public. The upper portion of the rudders was natural metal, while the rest of the aircraft was painted black. This, the ninth A-12, was lost along with its pilot Jack Weeks on June 5, 1968, due to an in-flight engine failure.

In a view of nine Blackbirds stored in a hangar at Palmdale, California, the second plane has a false tail number, painted in red: 77835. Its actual serial number was 60-6930. This was one of three A-12s marked with fake tail numbers during operations out of Kadena Air Base, Okinawa, during Project Black Shield, a year-long series of spy missions over North Vietnam in 1967 and 1968. This A-12 is now displayed at the US Space and Rocket Center, Huntsville, Alabama. *Tony Landis collection*

Lockheed A-12, serial number 60-6964, Article 121, is preserved on static display at the Air Force Flight Test Center Museum Annex, Blackbird Airpark, at Plant 42, Palmdale, California. This A-12 was the first of its model to fly, making its maiden flight on April 26, 1962. It logged a total of 322 flights. *David Dwight Jackson*

Red covers are installed to keep foreign objects out of the engine-air inlet on the A-12 at Palmdale. Under the right wing is an AG-330 start cart; its two engines drove a shaft that started the J58 jet engines. *David Dwight Jackson*

On display at the Southern Museum of Flight, in Birmingham, Alabama, is this Lockheed A-12, serial number 60-6937, also designated Article 131. This was one of several A-12s that flew spy missions over North Korea as part of Operation Black Shield, beginning in May 1967. *David Dwight Jackson*

A-12, serial number 60-6937, is observed from the front right. A red cover is visible inside the engine inlet. In the background is a North American F-100C Super Sabre. *David Dwight Jackson*

The right rudder of A-12, serial number 60-6937, is viewed from the right side. Below the tail number is the insignia of the Lockheed Skunk Works. The three pronounced panels forward of the exhaust nozzle are some of the pressure-actuated blow-in doors that admitted air to increase thrust in transonic flight. *David Dwight Jackson*

Displayed at the US Space and Rocket Center, Huntsville, Alabama, is Lockheed A-12, serial number 60-6930, Article 127. Like the A-12 preserved at the Southern Museum of Flight, this A-12 served in Operation Black Shield, flying ten missions in that program. *David Dwight Jackson*

The A-12 at Huntsville displays the chines whose forward ends blended without interruption into the nose of the aircraft, whereas the chines of the SR-71 had blunt front ends, aft of the nose. *David Dwight Jackson*

In a right-side view of the A-12 at Huntsville, the three blow-in doors (sometimes called suck-in doors) toward the rear of the engine nacelle, below the rudder, are in the open position. *David Dwight Jackson*

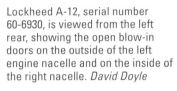

Lockheed A-12, serial number 60-6930, is viewed from the left rear, showing the open blow-in doors on the outside of the left engine nacelle and on the inside of the right nacelle. *David Doyle*

The left rudder, exhaust nozzle, outer wing, and blow-in doors are viewed close-up. The dark shapes toward the front of the engine nacelle are the forward and aft bypass doors. *David Doyle*

In a close-up view of the rear of the Huntsville A-12, toward the left is the tail cone of the fuselage, on the rear of which is the fuel vent, for dumping excess fuel before landing. At the center and the right is the right engine nacelle, with bypass doors toward the front, and blow-in doors and exhaust nozzle toward the rear. *David Doyle*

As seen from the rear, the rudders of the A-12 were canted inward, 15 degrees from vertical, principally to reduce the radar cross section (RCS) of the aircraft. The all-moving rudders were mounted on fixed stubs atop the engine nacelles, and the gaps between the bottoms of the rudders and the tops of the stubs are faintly visible. *David Doyle*

The pilot's windscreen and clamshell canopy are observed from the left side. The canopy and the windshield of the A-12s had dual-glass windows, with outer, monolithic glass panels separated from inner, laminated-glass panels by air gaps. The windows benefited from an internal hot-air defrosting and defogging system, an external rain-removal system, and deicing equipment. *David Doyle*

The nose landing gear of the A-12 at Huntsville, as seen from the left front, includes the landing and taxi lights. The tires lack the aluminum coloring of the original articles. *David Doyle*

In a frontal view of the left main landing gear, the tires have the aluminum coloring typical of the A-12's and SR-71's original tires. The outer fairing for the landing-gear bay, attached to the main gear, has a slight curve toward the bottom, to match the contour of the wing when the gear was retracted. *David Doyle*

One of the A-12s, Article 124, serial number 60-6927, was converted to an A-12 trainer. Nicknamed the "Titanium Goose," this plane had a cockpit for the instructor pilot, above and aft of the cockpit for the trainee. The "Titanium Goose" survives as a display plane at the California Science Center, Los Angeles.

CHAPTER 2

The Supersonic Mother-Daughter, the M/D-21

The M-21 was a purpose-built variant of the A-12 created for a singular purpose—to carry and launch the unmanned supersonic D-21 reconnaissance drone. Due to a US presidential decision to discontinue *manned* reconnaissance flights over certain foreign lands, the CIA began to look for alternatives. With satellite surveillance still years away, attention turned to drones. The project, code-named "Tagboard," led to the ramjet-powered D-21 drone, having a low radar cross section, 90,000-foot-plus altitude capabilities, and speeds over Mach 3.

The unmanned, single-use aircraft would carry a Hycon reconnaissance camera and other gear, which would be ejected postmission over international waters, where a Mid-Air Recovery System (MARS) would recover the package as it descended by parachute.

Since the ramjet of the D-21 had to ingest air at over Mach 1 to fire, it was decided that it would be launched from a variant of the only large aircraft capable of such speeds—the A-12. Two A-12 airframes were allocated to this project, Article 134 (60-6940) and Article 135 (60-6941). The A-12 and associated drone were designated M-21 (M = Mother) and D-21 (D = Daughter). In the fuselage compartment that on an A-12 normally held sensors, a second seat was installed for the launch control officer (LCO).

The first flight of the mother/daughter combination happened on December 22, 1964. Flight tests of the pair continued, and by May, speeds of Mach 2.6 had been attained, all with the daughter remaining attached. However, the desired launch speed was 3.1 Mach. On October 25, 1965, Kelly Johnson wrote, "We have had great difficulties in getting the M-21 to speed and range. We tried to run to Point Mugu for launch practice but could not make the range. Transonic acceleration is very poor, particularly with hot temperatures. As of this day, we are putting in 34,000-pound thrust engines. We are driving to a launch date of 15 November."

Finally, on March 3, 1966, the team was able to successfully launch a drone from Article 135. While the drone flew only 120 miles before crashing into Pacific, the launch itself was a success.

The length of the carrier pylon, necessarily short due to aerodynamics, meant that the M-21 had to fly a downward arc during launch so that the drone would clear the mother ship.

A second launch was made on April 27, again from Article 135, and this time the drone flew 1,200 miles before a hydraulic pump failed and the drone crashed into the sea.

By this time, even Kelly Johnson was advocating launching the D-21 from a B-52H, rather than M-21, stating that launching from the Stratofortress offered "greater safety, lower cost and greater deployment range."

A third launch from Article 135 was made on June 16, 1966, and it was the most successful yet, with the D-21 flying 1,600 miles and executing eight programmed turns.

The fourth launch, again from Article 135, was made on July 30 and proved disastrous. On this launch, the D-21 experienced an asymmetrical unstart, causing it to roll to the right and impact the right rudder of M-21 60-6941, with both aircraft traveling at Mach 3.25. The M-21 pitched up and its forward portion broke off. The entire sequence of events was recorded from Article 134, which was flying chase during the test.

Pilot Bill Park and LCO Ray Torick safely ejected, but Torick drowned in the Pacific after he mistakenly opened his helmet visor, causing his spacesuit-like flight suit to fill with water.

Following this accident, an August 15, 1966, meeting in Washington, DC, resulted in the cancellation of Project Tagboard, and following Kelly Johnson's recommendation, two B-52H bombers were modified to serve as launch platforms for rocket-equipped D-21 drones. The rockets pushed the D-21 up to speed to start the ramjet. The rocket-booster-equipped D-21s were designated D-21B.

The first of two M-21 mother aircraft for the D-21 ramjet-powered supersonic drones as it appeared while under construction in Burbank on August 23, 1963. The M-21s were purpose built from the outset, contrary to claims in some sources that they were A-12 conversions.

This was the first image of the M-21/D-21 combination released by the CIA, and it shows the first M-21, serial number 60-6940, in flight on December 22, 1964. Security concerns prevented this photo from being released for some eighteen years. This aircraft, although used extensively for flight testing with the drone in place, never actually launched a drone.

With the drone in place atop 60-6940, the close clearance between the D-21 and the rudders of the M-21 is apparent. The tight fit was of great concern to engineers, and for good reason, since the second M-21, serial number 60-6941, and its launch control officer, Ray Toriek, were lost when the drone collided with a rudder due to a partial unstart of the drone's engine.

The D-21 was mounted atop the M-21 fuselage via a pylon, clearly visible here. While wearing a natural-metal finish in this scene at Groom Dry Lake on December 22, 1964, the M-21 would, like most Blackbirds, be in time painted black.

An M/D-21 combination approaches a KC-135 for refueling, the latter's refueling boom visible at upper right. *Stan Piet collection*

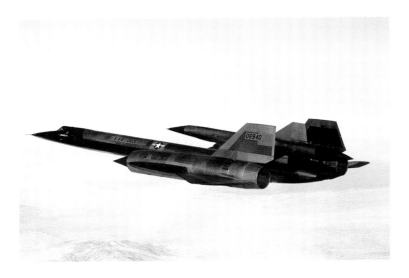

The sole remaining M-21, shown here on December 22, 1964, is today preserved at Seattle's Museum of Flight. But for the trainer, the M-21 was the first two-seat version of the Blackbird, with a launch control officer seated in the windowless Q-bay, an area normally occupied by reconnaissance gear in a conventional A-12.

The first of the two Lockheed M-21s, serial number 60-6940, is parked on a tarmac at Groom Lake, with a D-21 drone mounted on the dorsal pylon. Red protectors marked "NO STEP" are on the chines, to protect the delicate structures, and red protectors also are on the clear parts of the cockpit windscreen and canopy. *Lockheed via Tony Landis*

The Museum of Flight, Seattle, Washington, preserves the sole surviving Lockheed M-21, Article 134, serial number 60-6940. The other M-21, serial number 60-6941, was destroyed during a test flight in July 1966. Mounted atop the dorsal pylon on the aircraft is a D-21 drone, developed for performing unmanned reconnaissance missions. Under the bottoms of the landing-gear struts are supports, to bear the weight of the aircraft. *Tracy White*

A frontal view of the M-21 shows how the splines extend to the tip of the nose. In the background, the front of the D-21 drone is visible, resting on its pylon. *Tracy White*

The nose of the M-21, as well as the engine nacelles and the D-21 drone, is viewed from a lower perspective. In the foreground, attached to the tip of the nose, is the pitot tube, with the alpha/beta probe protruding from its left side. *Tracy White*

The M-21 has a two-tone finish, with black and unpainted metal areas. The pitot tube was unpainted metal. A small number '13" is stenciled in white on the nose. *Tracy White*

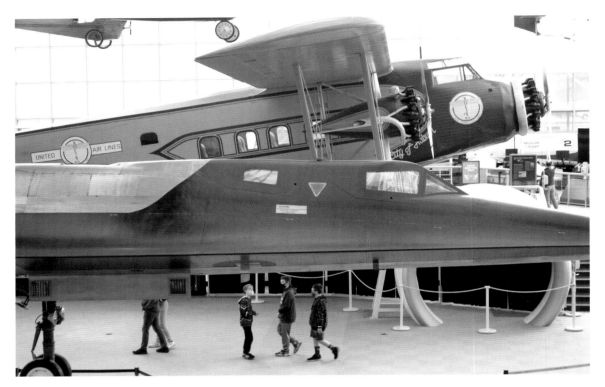

Between the cockpit canopies are yellow "RESCUE" and red-and-white ejector-seat warning stickers. In a dramatic example of how far aviation advanced from the 1930s to the 1960s, in the background is a Boeing 80A-1 trimotor transport plane, from 1934. *Tracy White*

In a view of the right side of the forward fuselage, the window on the canopy of the drone's launch control officer is visible. Two square ventilators are on the nose landing-gear door, forward and aft. *Tracy White*

The D-21 drone is poised between the rudders of the M-21 in this right-rear view. The blow-open doors on the engine nacelle below the rudder are open. Between the rudders and below the rear of the D-21 are the inner elevons and the tail cone. *Tracy White*

World War II technology meets highly advanced postwar tech in this photo of the M/D-21 next to a German V-1 flying bomb. The D-21 is painted overall in a matte black. Its pylon is visible below the craft. *Tracy White*

A full view of the outboard side of the right engine nacelle includes details of the spike, the forward and aft bypass doors, the blow-in doors, the rudder, and the exhaust nozzle. Below the wing is a start cart. *Tracy White*

The M-21 and D-21 combination is seen from the left rear, with views of the exhaust nozzles of the drone and the Blackbird. Below the left wing of the M-21 is a Pratt & Whitney J58 engine on an engine cart. *Tracy White*

The inner elevons are observed from below. Some of the corrugated skin is also noticeable. On the trailing edge at the upper center is the fuel vent. *Tracy White*

CHAPTER 3
Armed Speedster: The YF-12A

While both the A-12 and subsequent SR-71 were reconnaissance aircraft, a third variant of the Blackbird was unique in that it was to be an armed combat aircraft. Faced with concerns that hordes of Soviet bombers would strike North America, the Air Force sought an aircraft that could fly high enough and fast enough to intercept the Soviet bomber force long before it reached its target. It was desired that this interceptor had look-down, shoot-down capability.

The A-12 seemed to be an ideal starting point for such an aircraft, and in September 1960 work began on Project Kedlock, as the effort was designated, and the interceptor aircraft was initially known as the AF-12. The aircraft was to be so like the A-12 that the seventh through the ninth A-12 airframes were diverted to create the three interceptors.

The A-12, like all the Blackbird family, required a skilled pilot who had to simultaneously manage several systems to maintain flight and stay on course. The added demands of also operating weapons systems meant that a second seat would be required. For the AF-12, a second seat was added in what had been the A-12 sensor bay. This seat would be the station of the fire control system operator.

In the nose of the aircraft was installed a Hughes AN/ASG-18 fire-control system radar with 40-inch dish. The massive 1,380-pound AN/ASG-18 was the first US coherent-pulse Doppler radar with long-range look-down or look-up capability and was the most powerful such system in the world. To accommodate the system, the nose chines had to be cut back. The removal of the chines altered the aerodynamics of the aircraft, requiring the addition of ventral fins beneath the nacelles and a folding centerline fin beneath the rear fuselage.

On August 7, 1963, Lockheed test pilot Jim Eastham lifted the AF-12 into the air for the first time.

In a speech on February 29, 1964, President Johnson revealed the existence of the aircraft, referring to it as the "A-11" and without giving many specifics, but including releasing a limited number of photos of the AF-12. The president said, "The United States has successfully developed an advanced experimental jet aircraft, the A-11, which has been tested in sustained flight at more than 2,000 miles per hour and at altitudes in excess of 70,000 feet. The performance of the A-11 far exceeds that of any other aircraft in the world today. The development of this aircraft has been made possible by major advances in aircraft technology of great significance for both military and commercial applications. Several A-11 aircraft are now being flight[-]tested at Edwards Air Force Base in California. The existence of this program is being disclosed today to permit the orderly exploitation of this advanced technology in our military

Based on the A-12 airframe, the Lockheed YF-12A was an attempt to develop an advanced manned interceptor for the defense of the continental United States against Soviet threats other than the already well-defended routes over the Arctic areas. A McDonnell F-101B Voodoo chase plane accompanies the first A-12 as it vents fuel during a test flight out of Groom Lake. In available photos of this aircraft, no tail number is visible.

and commercial program." He continued, "The A-11 aircraft now at Edwards Air Force Base are undergoing extensive tests to determine their capabilities as long-range interceptors."

This announcement was made to obscure the fact that the A-12 even existed. Any sightings of the A-12 could be attributed as test flights of the A-11. Caught by surprise, program officials quickly dispatched two AF-12s from Groom Lake to Edwards Air Force Base.

By the time the weapons system was ready for testing, the aircraft had been redesignated YF-12A. Because the aircraft was "faster than a speeding bullet," armament was certainly going to be with missiles. Specifically, three AIM-47A air-to-air guided missiles would be carried in a bays beneath the aircraft. On April 16, 1964, one of the missiles, unpowered, was successfully ejected by a YF-12A in flight. On March 18, 1965, for the first time, an AIM-47 missile was fired from a YF-12A moving at Mach 3.2 at an altitude of 75,000 feet. Its target was 36 miles away and at 40,000 feet. The missile missed by 6 feet—a distance that still would have been lethal.

On the final test mission, September 21, 1966, while flying at Mach 3.2 at 74,000 feet, Article 1003 (YF-12A 60-6936) fired an unarmed missile at a QB-47 drone flying at 500 feet. The unarmed missile struck the QB-47, carrying away 4 feet of its left horizontal stabilizer.

Ultimately, seven missile firings were conducted from YF-12A aircraft, with all but one being deemed a success—the sole failure attributable to a malfunction in the missile.

The YF-12A had achieved all its objectives, and armed with this the Air Force approached Congress, requesting funding for ninety-three production F-12Bs, which was approved. On May 14, 1965, the Air Defense Command then placed the order with Lockheed, but the aircraft were not to materialize. Secretary of Defense Robert Strange McNamara refused to release the funds to produce the aircraft and continued this tactic for two more years. McNamara won this battle once and for all when on January 5, 1968, the Air Force sent Lockheed a letter instructing the company to destroy the tooling used to build the A-12/F-12/SR-71, thereby making the cost of further production of the aircraft increase substantially. Regarding this draconian step, later Kelly Johnson would write, "We have proceeded to store such items as are required for producing spare parts at Norton. The large jigs have been cut up for scrap and were finishing the clean-up of the complete area. Then years from now the country will be very sorry for taking the decision of stopping production on the whole Mach 3 series of aircraft in the USA." The tooling, which cost millions, returned $0.07 per pound to the US Treasury.

The first YF-12A flight ends with a smooth landing at Groom Dry Lake on August 7, 1963. Lockheed's YF-12 chief test pilot, Jim Eastham, was at the controls of the YF-12A; the drag chute has been deployed to slow the experimental fighter as an F-104 chase plane passes overhead. At this time, the bulk of the aircraft was a natural-metal color, with only a few components painted black. Later, all the aircraft of the A-12, M-21, YF-12A, and SR-71 families were painted black with a special heat-resistant, radar-scattering paint.

Armament was to consist of three AIM-47 very long-range guided missiles. Three YF-12As were produced. This example, serial number 60-6934, is equipped with camera pods on pylons underneath the engine nacelles. The YF-12A also had three ventral fins: two fixed outboard fins and a folding fin on the centerline. *National Archives*

YF-12A, serial number 60-6934, is parked on a tarmac. The buzz number on the engine nacelle, FX-934, includes the FX designator for the YF-12A and the last three digits of the serial number. The large, center dorsal fin is folded up. *National Archives*

The YF-12A is unveiled to the press for the first time, on September 30, 1964. Unlike the Lockheed A-12, the YF-12A's chines terminated a short distance forward of the cockpit windscreen, rather than terminating at a point at the front of the nose. *National Archives*

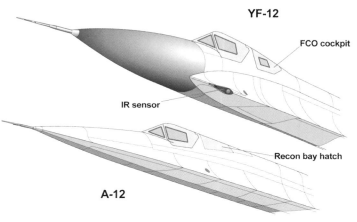

Differences between the forward fuselages of the A-12 and the YF-12A are illustrated. Infrared sensors were in the front ends of the truncated chines of the YF-12A, and this plane also had a rear cockpit for a fire-control officer (FCO).

Clarence "Kelly" Johnson (1910–90) poses in front of a YF-12A. In the late 1950s, Johnson became vice president of Lockheed's Advanced Development Projects (ADP), soon to be nicknamed the Skunk Works. In that capacity, he conceived, designed, and collaborated in numerous cutting-edge aeronautical projects, taking a key role in the development of the A-12, the YF-12A, and the SR-71. *National Archives*

A YF-12A is viewed from the front during its official rollout for the press at Edwards Air Force Base on September 30, 1964. The light-colored, dome-shaped infrared sensors on the blunt forward ends of the chines are visible from this angle. *National Archives*

The YF-12A was armed with three AIM-47A air-to-air guided missiles, one of which is on a cart next to a YF-12A. Originally designed to carry a conventional or nuclear warhead, by 1958 the nuclear warhead was dropped in favor of a high-explosive version. *National Museum of the United States Air Force*

The foreshortened chines that are characteristic of the YF-12A are clearly evident as one of the aircraft soars over a mountain range. *Stan Piet collection*

A YF-12A passes overhead during a test flight from Edwards Air Force Base, California, on September 30, 1964. The "USAF" and the border of the national insignia on the bottoms of the wings were painted in white. The large folding fin on the centerline of the aft fuselage appears to be lost in the shadows under the aircraft.

Lockheed YF-12A, serial number 60-6935, is performing a test flight over the desert. The plane's buzz number, FX-935, is marked in white on the upper part of the engine nacelle. The side window of the fire-control officer's cabin is visible, to the rear of the pilot's cockpit.

A YF-12A passes overhead during a test flight from Edwards Air Force Base, California, on September 30, 1964. The "USAF" and the border of the national insignia on the bottoms of the wings were painted in white. The large folding fin on the centerline of the aft fuselage appears to be lost in the shadows under the aircraft.

YF-12A, serial number 60-6936, rests at Edwards Air Force Base on June 29, 1970. Three white drawings of YF-12As on the fuselage below the pilot's windscreen represent world records set. This plane was lost following a fuel-line rupture on June 24, 1971. The crew survived.

YF-12A, serial number 60-6934, awaits its next mission at Edwards Air Force Base in about 1964. Streamlined camera pods are mounted below the engine nacelles. The buzz number, FX-934, is painted in white on the upper part of the right engine nacelle.

Sunlight and shadow highlight the snubbed front ends of the fuselage chines in this overhead view of YF-12A, USAF serial number 60-6936, on one of its test flights. The buzz number, FX-936, is faintly visible on the tops of the engine nacelles. Red stripes on the wings indicate permissible walkways. *Stan Piet collection*

The pilot's main instrument panel and the grip of his control stick (*bottom center*) are displayed in a YF-12A. At the top center of the panel is a radarscope, below which is an attitude directional indicator (ADI). In addition to dial gauges, there were vertical-tape instruments to the sides of the artificial horizon. The rudder pedals are in view below the instrument panel.

The YF-12A fire-control officer's instrument panel included controls for the Hughes AN/ASG-18 fire-control system. Speed and altitude tape gauges are to the sides of the two square map projectors on the center of the panel; at the bottom of the panel is a round radarscope.

BLACKBIRD SPECIFICATIONS

Model	A-12	YF-12A	SR-71A
Crew	1	2	2
Wingspan	54 feet, 7.4 inches	54 feet, 7.4 inches	54 feet, 7.4 inches
Length	102 feet	101 feet, 8 inches	107 feet, 5 inches
Height	18 feet, 4 inches	18 feet, 4 inches	18 feet, 6 inches
Empty Weight	38,000 pounds	68,000 pounds	56,500 pounds
Maximum Weight	117,000 pounds	124,000 pounds	145,000 pounds
Engine	2 × J-58	2 × J-58	2 × J-58
Maximum Range Unrefueled	2,500 miles	3,200 miles	3,200 miles
Maximum Altitude	95,000 feet	85,000 feet	89,500 feet
Maximum Speed	Mach 3.35 ~ 2,275 mph	Mach 3.24 ~ 2,185 mph	Mach 3.43 ~ 2,340 mph
First Flight	30 April 1962	7 August 1963	22 December 1964
Final Flight	21 June 1968	7 November 1979	9 October 1999

An unidentified technician, *left*, and NASA test pilot Earle O. Boyer examine a YF-12A wind-tunnel test model. NASA's Ames Research Center provided A-12 wind-tunnel test reports to NASA in 1967, and subsequently the Air Force provided NASA with two YF-12As for use as high-speed, high-altitude test aircraft. *National Archives*

NASA test pilot Earle O. Boyer poses with a YF-12A wind-tunnel test model. Fabricated from metal, the model was built to precise tolerances and was intended to facilitate the measurement of aerodynamic forces around the model at high wind speeds, replicating the aerodynamic effects of the actual YF-12A. *National Archives*

Two YF-12s transferred by the Air Force to NASA fly from Dryden Flight Research Center, Edwards Air Force Base, in 1975. To the right is YF-12A 60-6935, while to the left is YF-12C 60-6937, which actually was SR-71A 61-7951. The light-colored pod under the YF-12A, to the front of the camera pod, was part of the Cold Wall heat-transfer experiments. *NASA*

YF-12A number 2, serial number 60-6935, is parked on a tarmac at Edwards Air Force Base, California. This was during the period of 1969 to 1979, when the plane was assigned to NASA for high-speed flight tests and research. The canopy for the rear cockpit has been removed; aft of that cockpit is the refueling receptacle. The white circle-and-cross markings on the left wing were visual references for use in testing. The interior of the drag-chute doors and compartment is finished in a yellowish paint or zinc-chromate primer. Below the left wing is an engine-starter cart. *NASA via Tony Landis*

The NASA YF-12C makes a test flight over mountainous terrain. The NASA tail number, 60-6937, was a bogus one, being the next number in sequence after the three YF-12As. In reality, there was no such thing as a YF-12C. This designation was created because NASA had lost one of their YF-12As, and the only thing available to replace it was an SR-71A, an aircraft the Soviets did not know yet existed. *NASA*

In December 1969, the US Air Force transferred this YF-12A, serial number 60-6935, to NASA at the Dryden Flight Research Center at Edwards Air Force Base. Ten years later, in 1975, the plane found a permanent home at the US Air Force Museum at Wright-Patterson Air Force Base, Ohio. *Stan Piet collection*

The National Museum of the US Air Force has preserved YF-12A, serial number 60-6935, since November 1979, when it was flown to the museum's location at Wright-Patterson Air Force Base, Ohio. It is the only survivor of the three YF-12As.

A tow bar is attached to the nose landing gear of the National Museum of the US Air Force's YF-12A. The irregular shape on the forward end of the chine, directly below the cockpit canopy, represents the location of an infrared sensor.

In mid-October 2015, the YF-12A was moved into a recently finished building at the National Museum of the US Air Force. Here, a tractor is using a tow bar to push the aircraft into the building. Inside the door of the building is a Titan IV missile. In the background are, *left*, Hawker Siddeley XV-6A Kestrel, serial number 64-18262, and, *right*, North American X-10, serial number 51-9307. Both of these planes would also take up residence in the new building.

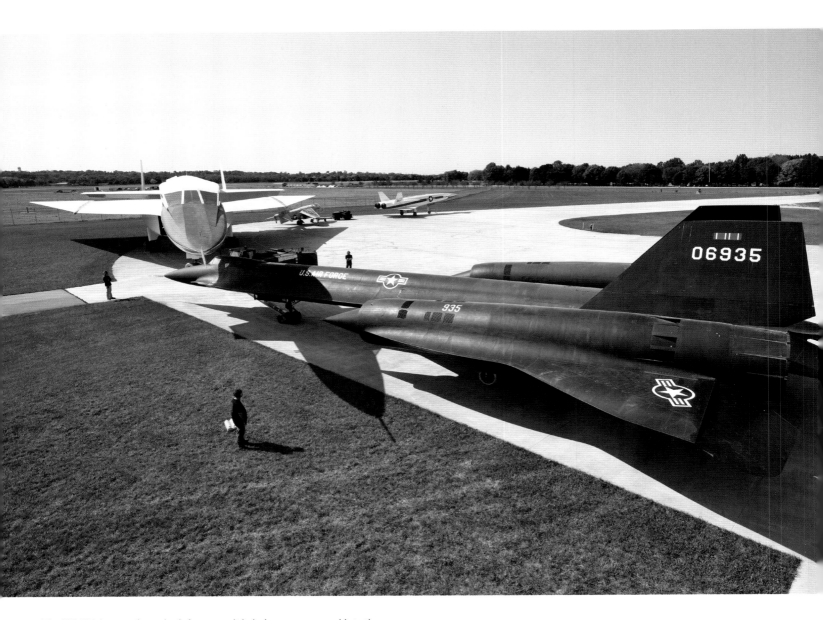

The YF-12A is seen from the left rear as it is being maneuvered into the new building at the museum. In the background is the first of the two North American XB-70 Valkyries, which would be moved into the building, next to the YF-12A.

The inboard and outboard elevons are depressed in this photo of the moving of the YF-12A into the new building. The red, white, and blue device above the tail number is the US Air Force Distinguished Unit Award ribbon.

The YF-12A is being spotted into its space in the new building in October 2015. A good view is available of the left afterburner and the exhaust outlet, or "turkey feathers."

CHAPTER 4

Go Fast or Go Home: The SR-71

While the CIA was acquiring the A-12, the Air Force was eager for its own high-speed, high-altitude reconnaissance aircraft. The service considered a variant of the supersonic XB-70 Valkyrie, dubbed the RS-70, but quickly decided that the CIA's A-12 held greater potential. Further, by cooperating with the CIA, the Air Force would benefit from lower costs, thanks to the use of much of the same production tooling—and obviously much of the research and development—as the agency. In March 1962 the CIA approved the Air Force's issuing of a study contract to Lockheed.

Ironically, while at this time the Air Force coveted the manned strategic reconnaissance operations, three decades later they eschewed this task, leading to the end of the SR-71 program, to the dismay of much of the nation's (and allies') intelligence network.

The Air Force version was initially known as the R-12 (derived from A-12), then later the RS-71 (building on the aborted Valkyrie-based RS-70 predecessor), but Air Force chief of staff Curtis LeMay successfully lobbied for an "SR" designation, indicative of strategic reconnaissance. A popular myth, based on a press release about the speech, is that President Johnson misspoke during a July 24, 1964, address, referring to the aircraft as SR-71 rather than RS-71, but in fact a review of Johnson's original notes and speech, and recordings of the speech, prove he said SR-71, but the stenographer preparing the press release mistakenly typed RS-71.

The Air Force version was to be slightly longer, allowing additional fuel and intelligence-gathering equipment to be carried—as well as a second crewman, the reconnaissance systems officer (RSO). Of course, this led to the aircraft being heavier than the A-12. As a result, the A-12 could fly slightly higher, and slightly faster, than the SR-71 would be able to.

Air Force personnel inspected a mockup on June 13–14, 1963, and the design was refined and given a final review on December 11. Construction of the initial order for six aircraft began thereafter, with the first aircraft being trucked from the Burbank factory and traveling to Palmdale, arriving on October 29, 1964. On December 22, 1964, Lockheed test pilot Bob Gilliland took the aircraft into the air for the first time.

The contrasting colors seen along the outer edges of the airframes of these three SR-71s on the assembly line are indicative of the radar-absorbing materials used in these areas, compared to the titanium that composed most of the rest of the aircraft.

The week prior, the Strategic Air Command had announced that the SR-71s would be assigned to the 4200th Strategic Reconnaissance Wing, which would be based at the 22,000-acre Beale Air Force Base outside Marysville, California, about 25 miles north of Sacramento. The Air Force allocated $8.4 million for facilities construction for the new wing.

Flight crews for the wing were recruited from U-2 and B-58 units. As a rule, SR-71 pilots and RSO teams trained together and then served together throughout their time in the SR-71.

The SR-71 entered service in January 1966. During the Vietnam War, SR-71 overflights averaged one per day, during which time the enemy unsuccessfully fired 800 surface-to-air missiles against the aircraft. Ultimately, throughout the career of the aircraft, a reported 4,500-plus missiles were fired at the aircraft, none of them being successful at downing or even damaging the Blackbird.

By the late 1980s, the Air Force wanted to shelve the expensive-to-operate SR-71 to free up funding for other projects. These efforts were thwarted by Congress until 1989, when the aircraft's detractors, among them Air Force chief of staff Gen. Larry D. Welch, got their way, and SAC ordered the type to be retired and placed in storage. January 26, 1990, was scheduled to be the final day for SR-71 flights. Lt. Col. Rod Dyckman, the 1st Strategic Reconnaissance Squadron commander, and his RSO, Lt. Col. Tom Bergam, flew the final mission, making multiple passes over Beale AFB.

On March 6, 1990, two months after the official retirement of the SR-71, Article 2023, serial number 61-7972, was readied for flight—a one-way trip to Dulles International Airport outside Washington, DC, for delivery to the Smithsonian's National Air and Space Museum. The aircraft, flown by Lt. Col. Ed Yeilding with his RSO, Lt. Col. Joe "J. T." Vida, set four international speed records during the flight, including fastest time from Los Angeles to Washington—sixty-four minutes, twenty seconds, at an average speed of 2,176 mph.

However, there were many in Congress who were not pleased with the retirement of the iconic aircraft, including influential Senator John Glenn, who the next day soundly chastised the Air Force and the president for what he viewed as a shortsighted decision to retire what remained the nation's most versatile intelligence-gathering asset.

Glenn was not alone in his position, and by 1995, aided by Senators Byrd, Stevens, and Nunn, he persuaded Congress to direct that the SR-71 program be reactivated. An appropriation of $100 million was provided to return three of the aircraft to the sky. Complying with the order, the Air Force reactivated the SR-71B trainer 61-7956 and two SR-71As, 61-7967 and 61-7971. The unit would fly from Edwards, where NASA was still flying Blackbirds, to control expenses, rather than returning to the traditional SR-71 home of Beale AFB.

The SR-71s were upgraded to include the latest in electronics, including new data links and real-time imagery. Additionally, electrical-optical capabilities were added to the imaging systems. Despite these improvements, and the congressional mandate, the detractors in the service still had the upper hand—they simply refused to utilize the aircraft; accordingly, the $100 million expenditure produced no strategic results. Thus, when the White House directed the Air Force to cut spending, the Air Force offered the SR-71 to President Clinton. Accordingly, his line-item veto of $39 million for the SR-71 programs of October 15, 1997, halted all USAF SR-71 flights.

At the Lockheed Flight Test Center in Palmdale, the first SR-71A, serial number 61-7950, is being prepared for its black paint job just prior to its first flight on December 22, 1964.

Following the application of the black paint job and the US Air Force markings, the first SR-71 was prepared for its first flight. Here, the nose of the aircraft has been removed to allow the installation of test instruments for that flight.

Lockheed test pilot Robert J. Gilliland was the first man to fly the SR-71. He is seen here wearing the first-generation pressure suit worn by SR-71 pilots. At his feet is a portable air conditioner.

Model	Lockheed number	USAF number
	1	2
A-12	121	60-6924
A-12	122	60-6925
A-12	123	60-6926*
A-12B	124	60-6927
A-12	125	60-6928*
A-12	126	60-6929*
A-12	127	60-6930
A-12	128	60-6931
A-12	129	60-6932*
A-12	130	60-6933
A-12	131	60-6937
A-12	132	60-6938
A-12	133	60-6939*
YF-12A	1001	60-6934*
YF-12A	1002	60-6935
YF-12A	1003	60-6936*
M-21	134	60-6940
M-21	135	60-6941*
SR-71A	2001	61-7950*
SR-71A	2002	61-7951
SR-71A	2003	61-7952*
SR-71A	2004	61-7953*
SR-71A	2005	61-7954*
SR-71A	2006	61-7955
SR-71B	2007	61-7956
SR-71B	2008	61-7957*
SR-71A	2009	61-7958
SR-71A	2010	61-7959
SR-71A	2011	61-7960
SR-71A	2012	61-7961
SR-71A	2013	61-7962
SR-71A	2014	61-7963
SR-71A	2015	61-7964
SR-71A	2016	61-7965*
SR-71A	2017	61-7966*
SR-71A	2018	61-7967
SR-71A	2019	61-7968
SR-71A	2020	61-7969*
SR-71A	2021	61-7970*
SR-71A	2022	61-7971
SR-71A	2023	61-7972
SR-71A	2024	61-7973
SR-71A	2025	61-7974*
SR-71A	2026	61-7975
SR-71A	2027	61-7976
SR-71A	2028	61-7977*
SR-71A	2029	61-7978*
SR-71A	2030	61-7979
SR-71A	2031	61-7980
SR-71C	2000	61-7981

* Aircraft destroyed in accident. No Blackbirds were ever lost due to enemy action. Four Blackbird crewmen were killed in the twenty incidents above.

Seen here in flight in about 1966, the first SR-71A, USAF serial number 61-7950, made its maiden flight on December 22, 1964. The long-range strategic reconnaissance aircraft was lost at Edwards Air Force Base on January 10, 1967, during tests of an antiskid brake system; the pilot survived. There were a total of thirty-two SR-71s: twenty-nine were standard SR-71As, two were SR-71B two-seat trainers, and one, an SR-71C trainer, was a composite aircraft constructed from the wing and rear fuselage of YF-12A 60-6934 and the forward fuselage of a static-test aircraft. *National Archives*

An SR-71A rests on a tarmac in 1964 or 1965. The tail number is indistinct, but the next-to-last digit appears to be 5, indicating a serial number in the 61-7950 to -17959 range. The similarities between this and the following photo suggest this was SR-71A 61-7950. *National Archives*

The right front of SR-71A 61-7950 is seen in 1964 or 1965, before the SR-71As became operational and prior to their first assignments to Beale Air Force Base in California. *National Archives*

As seen in this photo of 61-7950, the SR-71As retained the general shape of the A-12. The SR-71A, however, had a longer tail cone on the rear of the fuselage, was heavier, and had a second cockpit behind the pilot's cockpit for a reconnaissance systems officer (RSO). *National Archives*

Undergoing a test flight, the first SR-71A wings its way high above the California desert. The light-colored shape on the underside of the chine below the RSO's cockpit is a white marking around the UHF antenna, used during domestic flights. *National Archives*

The contours of the SR-71A's right rear section are in view on an airfield tarmac. As was the case with the Lockheed A-12 and the YF-12A, the rudders canted inward. On the SR-71A, the cant was at an angle of 15 degrees from vertical. *National Archives*

The fifth SR-71A, USAF serial number 64-17954, soars above a desert landscape, affording a clear view of the extended tail cone. Following an aborted takeoff and a fire at Edwards Air Force Base, this plane was written off on April 11, 1969. *National Archives*

The spikes in the engine inlets were moved forward and aft in order to optimize airflow, according to the aircraft's speed and altitude. This left spike is shown in the full-forward position. This was the position of the spikes at subsonic speeds. *Lockheed via Tony Landis*

The spike was moved aft through hydraulic power, as shown here, as the aircraft accelerated above Mach 1, preventing supersonic air from entering the engine, and controlling the flow of air through the throat of the inlet. Bypass louvers on the nacelles acted in concert with the spikes to control the airflow. *Lockheed via Tony Landis*

The left spike is viewed from another angle, retracted farther into the inlet. Because of these variable-geometry inlets, over 80 percent of the thrust was produced by the inlet at Mach 3.2, and 20 percent was from the engines. *Lockheed via Tony Landis*

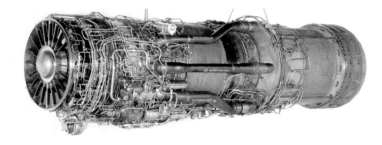

This is the YJ58, the service test version of the J58 engine. The YJ58 had some gold-plated components, as seen here, and was used in the A-12 and early YF-12A aircraft. Later aircraft used the standardized J58 (Pratt & Whitney model JT11D-20), which was essentially identical, albeit lacking the gold plating. The engines, which weighed 6,500 pounds each, developed 30,000 to 34,000 pounds of thrust, depending on specific submodels.

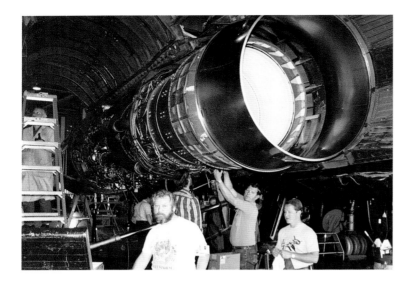

Lockheed mechanics are installing a Pratt & Whitney J58 jet engine into the left nacelle of an SR-71. Introduced in 1956, the J58 was used in the A-12s, YF-12A, and SR-71. It was the first dual-cycle jet engine to enter service, and at speeds from Mach 2 and up, it functioned as a ramjet engine. *Lockheed via Tony Landis*

Each engine nacelle and outer wing panel of the SR-71 composed a unit, hinged to the top of the inboard half of the nacelle. The outer half of the nacelle and the outer wing panel could be unlocked and swung up to allow full access to the engine. A Blackbird is shown with the engine removed and the outer half of the nacelle and the outer right wing swung up. Toward the upper left is the right rudder. *Lockheed via Tony Landis*

The SR-71A in this head-on view appears to be the first one, USAF serial number 61-7950. Of interest are the shape of the pilot's cockpit windscreen and the configurations of the landing-gear wheels: dual wheels on the nose gear and triple wheels on each main gear. Two landing lights are on the nose-gear strut, a small one at the center and a larger one on the right side of the strut. *National Archives*

In an overhead view of an SR-71A with a white band painted around the nose, the dark feature to the rear of the RSO's cockpit is the round window for the astronavigation system (ANS). Aft of the ANS window, the rectangular, recessed feature is the aerial-refueling receptacle. The shape of the chine around the forward part of the fuselage is apparent. *National Archives*

SR-71A, USAF serial number 61-7967, lifts off a runway at Edwards Air Force Base on April 27, 1967. This plane, which later served with the 9th Strategic Reconnaissance Wing into the mid-1980s, now is preserved at the Eighth Air Force Museum in Louisiana. *National Archives*

The same SR-71A, USAF serial number 61-7967, is seen from the left side during takeoff from Edwards Air Force Base on April 27, 1967. This plane, which was rolled out on April 18, 1966, eventually amassed a total of 2,765.5 flight hours. *National Archives*

SR-71A, serial number 61-7960, goes through its paces on its own test flight from Edwards. The national insignia on the fuselage features a white border. *National Archives*

SR-71A, serial number 61-7977, was lost in this takeoff accident at Beale Air Force Base on October 10, 1968. A wheel assembly of the main landing gear had failed, causing the aircraft to leave the runway and impact a drainage ditch.

The RSO, Capt. James A. Kogler, ejected, but the pilot, Major Gabriel Kardong, stayed with the aircraft. Both men survived without injury. While the SR-71A was written off after this accident, the cockpit of the aircraft survives today as a display at the Museum of Flight.

Seen on a tarmac is an SR-71A; the indistinct tail number appears to be 17950, equivalent to USAF serial number 61-7950. The white band around the nose is consistent with the one seen in other photos of serial number 61-7950.
National Archives

An SR-71 prepares for a mission at Beale Air Force Base, California, sometime during 1969. Compared to the contours of the A-12 and the YF-12A, this aircraft features chines whose front ends are fuller and less tapered. *National Archives*

An SR-71A takes off from Beale Air Force Base in 1969. This facility, 40 miles north of Sacramento, had been the home to the operational SR-71s since January 1966, first under the 4200th Strategic Reconnaissance Wing (SRW) and then, starting in June 1966, the 9th SRW. *National Archives*

On a flight out of Beale Air Force Base in 1969, SR-71A, USAF serial number 61-7953, wings its way above the snow-capped Sierra Nevada mountains. A large white cross and the last three digits of the tail number are emblazoned on the side of the engine nacelle. *National Archives*

Sunlight reflects off the left side of SR-71A, 61-7953 during a flight. Very faintly visible above the tail number on each rudder is a depiction of the red, white, and blue ribbon of the Air Force Outstanding Unit Award. *National Archives*

Clad in pressure suits, SR-71A crewmen prepare to enter their aircraft prior to a flight at Beale Air Force Base in 1969. Made by the David Clark Company, the suits were essential for life support at the high altitudes at which the SR-71 operated. *National Archives*

In an incident similar to that which caused the loss of 61-7977, 61-7954 was lost when a tire and wheel failed during a maximum-gross-weight takeoff at Edwards Air Force Base on April 11, 1969. Although appearing minimally damaged, in fact 7954 was badly damaged by fire. Subsequently, aluminum alloy wheels replaced the flammable magnesium wheels, eliminating this problem.

Lockheed SR-71A, serial number 61-7969, was an ill-fated Blackbird. In May 1970, while conducting an operational reconnaissance mission from Kadena Air Base, Okinawa, Japan, this plane crashed in Thailand as a result of a stall. Both crewmen successfully ejected and survived. *National Archives*

The second of the SR-71As, Article 2002 and USAF serial number 61-7951, saw service with NASA starting in 1971. For deception purposes during its stint with NASA, the plane was redesignated YF-12C and was assigned a spurious serial number, "borrowed" from one of the A-12s: 60-6937. The plane is shown at Edwards Air Force Base. It currently is displayed at the Pima Air and Space Museum, in Arizona.

On February 14, 1972, two crewmen about to take their first flight together pose with an SR-71A at Beale Air Force Base. SR-71 crews wore several types of continually improved pressure suits made by the David Clark Company over the decades. *National Archives*

On the rudder of SR-71, serial number 61-7974, of the 8th Strategic Reconnaissance Wing in 1972 are a red numeral 1 and an image of a Habu—a venomous Okinawan snake that SR-71 pilots adopted as their nickname, below which is "Ichi Ban," Japanese for "Number 1." *National Archives*

An SR-71 undergoes maintenance in a hangar at Beale Air Force Base in August 1972. At any given time, typically 20 percent of the twenty-five operational SR-71s were down for maintenance; thus, usually sixteen SR-71s were available for service. *National Archives*

In order to start the J58 engines, they first had to be turning at 3,200 rpm. When the A-12 first entered service, this activation was accomplished through the use of an AG330 "Start Cart," which housed a pair of Buick 401-cubic-inch-displacement V-8 engines. These engines drove a gearbox through a 12-inch-wide belt. A probe from the gearbox engaged the drive pad on the J58. *James Goodall*

The AG330 Start Cart was a necessary accessory for powering up the Blackbird's J58 jet engines. Initially, the AG330 contained two side-by-side Buick 401-cubic-inch V-8 engines with automatic transmissions, developing 400 hp. The engines powered a vertical shaft that was attached to the starter on the bottom of the J58 engine. The Buick Wildcat engines were replaced with Chevrolet LS-7 454 engines in the mid-1970s; the example seen here is a Buick Wildcat. *Tracy White*

With the access panel open on the AG330, one of the two Buick Wildcat engines is in view. Engine air is provided through a flex hose and a metal elbow. The yellow box to the left was for storing manuals and report. *Tracy White*

The Buick Wildcat is viewed from a different perspective. Yellow ignition wires lead to the tan-colored distributor. The four right exhausts are rust colored; they were routed to a straight tailpipe, with no muffler. To the front of the engine are the alternator, the fan belt, and the fan. *Tracy White*

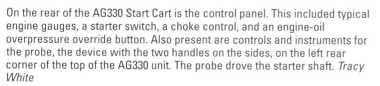

On the rear of the AG330 Start Cart is the control panel. This included typical engine gauges, a starter switch, a choke control, and an engine-oil overpressure override button. Also present are controls and instruments for the probe, the device with the two handles on the sides, on the left rear corner of the top of the AG330 unit. The probe drove the starter shaft. *Tracy White*

The Buick engines were contemporaneous with the introduction of the aircraft. Over time, parts availability became a problem, and a revised AG330 powered by a pair of Chevrolet LS-7 454-cubic-inch-displacement V-8 engines came into use. The starting procedure was the same. In well-developed fields, a special Garret low-pressure air starter was used, relying on a high-volume 60 psi motor to turn the J-58. *James Goodall*

Ground crewmen make final adjustments to SR-71A, serial number 61-7963, prior to a flight at Beale Air Force Base in August 1972. A red cover with a "remove before takeoff" streamer is over the pitot tube on the nose. This aircraft survives and is on static display at Beale. *National Archives*

An SR-71 soars overhead on its way out of Beale Air Force Base in August 1972. Although numerous enemy fighter planes attempted to intercept SR-71s over the years, none ever got close enough to enjoy a view such as this one. *National Archives*

Ground crewmen prepare SR-71A, serial number 61-7983, for engine run-up. These images were taken at Beale Air Force Base between August 10 and 13, 1972. Evidence that this aircraft was USAF serial number 61-7963 lies in the red windshield cover and the red engine-intake covers, which are marked in white with the last three digits of the plane's USAF serial number, 963. *National Archives*

Sometime during 1972 at Beale Air Force Base, an SR-71A with an indistinct tail number taxis past a flight line of KC-135 tankers, with a B-52 bomber in the foreground. The SR-71s were serviced by a fleet of thirty-five Boeing KC-135Q tankers based at Beale. *National Archives*

An SR-71A takes off from Beale Air Force Base during 1972. The SR-71A required approximately 4,400 feet of runway. Once clear of the runway, the plane climbed at a speed of 400 knots and then went supersonic, preferably over an unpopulated area. *National Archives*

SR-71, USAF serial number 61-7974, cruises at fairly low altitude above the Central Valley of California in 1972. This plane was a veteran of the SR-71's 1968 deployment to Kadena Air Base on Okinawa and was marked "Ichi Ban" on the rudders. *National Archives*

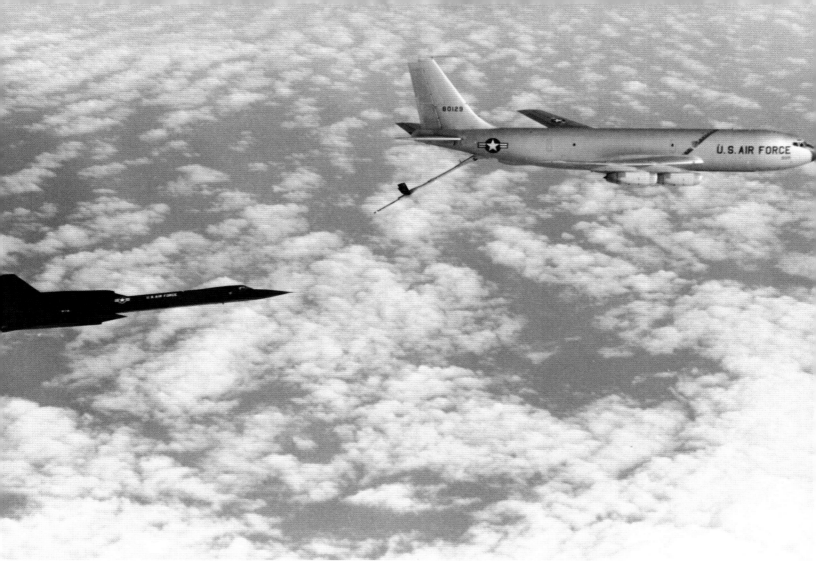

During a flight out of Beale Air Force Base, California, in 1972, an SR-71A approaches the lowered refueling boom of a KC-135 tanker. This Blackbird, serial number 61-1798, was nicknamed Rapid Rabbit and sported a white Playboy Bunny on the rudder. *National Archives*

On September 20, 1973, Senator Barry Goldwater and President Richard M. Nixon present the 1972 Harmon International Trophy to Lieutenant Colonels Thomas B. Estes and Dewain C. Vick for their record-breaking nonstop flight in an SR-71A in April 1971. *National Museum of the United States Air Force*

During the October 1973 Yom Kippur War, the US Air Force conducted long-range strategic reconnaissance missions over the Middle East, using SR-71s based in New York State. This example, serial number 61-9764, is shown at Plattsburgh, New York, on a snowy day in late 1973. *National Museum of the United States Air Force*

An SR-71A is on display at an air show in 1974. To the front of the aircraft are signs indicating that the plane is assigned to the 9th Strategic Reconnaissance Wing at Beale Air Force Base. Red covers are on the canopies, tires, engine inlets, and other openings. *National Archives*

The chines of an SR-71A are displayed to dramatic effect in 1974. The chines not only improved the plane's flight stability and low-speed maneuverability but also offered space for reconnaissance and electronic equipment, including a battery of recon cameras. *National Archives*

In this view of SR-71A, serial number 61-7975, parked on an airfield tarmac in 1974, the horizontal splits between the lower, fixed, parts of the rudders and the movable upper parts are clearly visible. The upper parts of the rudders swiveled as a whole unit. *National Archives*

This Blackbird SR-71A, serial number 61-9795, is observed from the left rear. By the time this photo was taken in 1974, it had one rudder salvaged from SR-71A 61-7978. Currently, this Blackbird is on static display at March Air Reserve Base, California. *National Archives*

Seen from the rear, the SR-71A impresses with its space-age contours. Also obvious is the distinction between the fixed lower parts of the rudders and the movable upper parts. The sign in the foreground warns that this is a restricted area. *National Archives*

SR-71A, serial number 61-7959, was modified with an extended rear fuselage. The 8-foot extension, which earned the aircraft the appellation "Big Tail," housed various combinations of reconnaissance equipment and sensors, including the optical bar camera (OBC). The tail extension, horizontal in flight, was raised during takeoff and landing to prevent ground strikes. *Lockheed via Tony Landis*

The Big Tail first flew on December 3, 1974, and made its last flight on October 29, 1976, before being placed in storage. With the US withdrawal from Vietnam, the perceived need that led to the Big Tail development had abated. At the conclusion of USAF Blackbird operations in 1991, the aircraft was trucked to the Armament Museum at Eglin Air Force Base, where it remains on display.

Having just set a new transatlantic speed record, SR-71, serial number 61-7972, of the 9th Strategic Reconnaissance Wing approaches Farnborough Airport, England, on September 1, 1974. The New York–London flight took approximately one hour, fifty-five minutes. *National Archives*

A light-colored border delineates the rectangular refueling-receptacle door to the rear of the aft cockpit in this overhead view of SR-71A, serial number 61-7961, in flight in 1974. Red lines on the fuselage and inner wing sections mark out the walkways. *National Archives*

Lockheed SR-71, USAF serial number 61-7972, is about to land at Farnborough at the end of its September 1, 1974, New York–London flight. For this mission, the pilot was Maj. James Sullivan, and the RSO was Maj. Noel Widdifield.
National Archives

The drag chute has been deployed on SR-71A, USAF serial number 61-7972, as it touches down at Farnborough on September 1, 1974. The occasion of the record-breaking transatlantic flight coincided with the opening day of the Farnborough Air Show. *National Museum of the United States Air Force*

SR-71A, serial number 61-7972, is parked at Farnborough after its transatlantic flight. Although the New York–London part of the flight was the one that counted for the record books, the flight was a nonstop one that originated at Beale Air Force Base, California. *National Archives*

Noel Widdifield, *left*, and James Sullivan, *on the phone*, receive a congratulatory message from President Gerald Ford following their record-setting transatlantic flight on September 1, 1974. In the black pinstripe suit is Senator John Tower of Texas. *National Museum of the United States Air Force*

The crew of SR-71, serial number 61-7972, greet the press upon exiting from their plane upon arrival at the Farnborough Air Show, September 1, 1974. The pilot, Maj. James Sullivan, is to the left, and his RSO, Maj. Noel Widdifield, is to the right. This photograph offers some close-up details of the pressure suits as worn by SR-71 crewmen in the mid-1970s. The rings on the suits at neck level are fittings for the helmets. *National Museum of the United States Air Force*

The operations and maintenance crews supporting SR-71A 61-7972's New York–London speed run on September 1, 1974, pose next to the plane with a placard celebrating the unit, the crew, Lockheed's connection, and the time and speed of the flight. *National Museum of the United States Air Force*

In a photo of an SR-71A landing at Ellsworth Air Force Base, South Dakota, in July 1975, one of the three drag chutes (probably the extraction chute) has been jettisoned and is floating to Earth while the main drag chute has been deployed. *National Archives*

An SR-71A assigned to the 9th Strategic Reconnaissance Wing taxis to its hangar at Kadena Air Base, Okinawa, on August 15, 1975. In the years following the end of the Vietnam War, SR-71As out of Kadena continued to fly recon missions to Asia. *National Archives*

SR-71A, serial number 61-7961, is seen in flight during 1976. During the preceding year this Blackbird had been involved in poststrike reconnaissance of a US attack on Koh Tang, an island off the Cambodian Coast, as part of a successful mission to free the crew of SS *Mayaguez*. *National Archives*

Lockheed SR-71A, USAF serial number 61-7963, cruises at relatively high altitude during a flight out of Kadena Air Base, Okinawa, in 1976. This aircraft served two rotations to Kadena: August 21, 1972, to June 13, 1973, and August 13, 1975, to July 16, 1976. *National Archives*

Its landing gear partially retracted, SR-71A, serial number 61-7958, flies over the California countryside in 1976. During that year, manned by Capt. Eldon Joersz and Maj. George Morgan, this plane would establish a speed record of 2,193 miles per hour. *National Archives*

Lockheed SR-71A, USAF serial number 61-7958, chalks up some flying time in 1976. Later, from July 27 to 28 that year, the aircraft took part in attempts at new speed records. It had been the first mission-capable SR-71 delivered to the Air Force. *National Archives*

SR-71, USAF serial number 61-7958, set two world and class records for speed in July 1976: over a 1,000-kilometer closed circuit at 2,092.29 miles per hour, and over a 15/25-kilometer straight course at a speed of 2,193.167 miles per hour. *National Archives*

Two SR-71As participated in the July 27–28, 1976, attempts at speed and altitude records: 61-7958, seen in the preceding several photographs, and 61-7963. This image shows one of the two SR-71As at that time, with a large white cross on it to aid in tracking. *National Archives*

The landing gear is lowered on SR-71, serial number 61-9758, around the time of the July 27–28, 1976, attempts at new speed and altitude records. The two Blackbirds used in the attempts tried to break six existing world records but succeeded in breaking only three. *National Archives*

SR-71, serial number 61-9758, is viewed from a different perspective as it makes a landing approach during the July 27–28, 1976, attempts on the speed and altitude records. The last three digits of the aircraft's serial number were marked in white on the engine nacelles. *National Archives*

This US Air Force publicity photo of SR-71A, serial number 61-7958, flying above a lake in California was taken in advance of this plane's July 1976 attempts to gain new speed records. The red stripe delineating a walkway is visible on the fuselage. *National Archives*

Retraction of the landing gear has commenced on SR-71A, serial number 61-7958, as it takes off from Andrews Air Force Base, Maryland, in July 1976. The occasion was an air show. A dull-red glow of afterburner flame is faintly visible aft of each of the jet exhausts. *National Archives*

SR-71A, serial number 61-7958, approaches to land during an air show at Andrews Air Force Base in July 1976. Landing the big, fast SR-71A at a busy airfield such as Andrews required skilled coordination with ground controllers and a strict descent profile. *National Archives*

A "follow-me" pickup truck takes its position to the front of an SR-71A, most likely serial number 61-7958, which has just landed at Andrews Air Force Base, Maryland, during an air show held in July 1976. Heat shimmer is visible to the rear of the Blackbird. *National Archives*

The SR-71A has come to a halt at Andrews Air Force Base in July 1976, and ground crewmen are readying a deplaning ramp for the aircrew. Seen from the front, an SR-71 could appear much more compact than it really was. *National Archives*

Ground crewmen on the top of the deplaning ramp are standing by at Andrews Air Force Base, ready to assist the pilot and the reconnaissance systems officer of SR-71A, serial number 61-7958, to exit the cockpit. Both of the cockpit hatches are still closed. *National Archives*

Taken moments after the preceding photograph, both cockpit hatches of SR-71A, USAF serial number 612-9758, are now open, and the pilot and the RSO will soon be deplaning. Both of the aircrewmen still have their white helmets on. *National Archives*

A Lockheed U-2R ultra-high-altitude reconnaissance plane of the 349th Strategic Reconnaissance Squadron flies past SR-71A, serial number 61-7962, assigned to the 1st Strategic Reconnaissance Squadron, at Beale Air Force Base, California, on March 10, 1977. *National Archives*

Seen in flight in January 1978, SR-71A, USAF serial number 61-7964, had an operational career that began with its first flight on May 11, 1966, and concluded with its final flight on March 20, 1990. It survives as a display aircraft at the Strategic Air and Space Museum in Nebraska.

Lockheed SR-71A, serial number 62-7964, is viewed from above during a flight over mountainous terrain. The dark-colored rectangles on the forward parts of the engine nacelles are engine-intake bleed doors, which helped regulate the flow of air into and out of the inlets. *National Archives*

The same SR-71A shown in the two preceding photos, serial number 61-7964, banks left above Beale Air Force Base, California, in 1978. *National Archives*

A Lockheed SR-71A takes off from an undisclosed base sometime during 1979. The glare of a landing light is visible on the nose-gear strut. Having only just lifted off the runway, the landing gear is already being retracted. *National Archives*

In July 1979, an SR-71A assigned to the 1st Strategic Reconnaissance Squadron takes off from Beale Air Force Base, California, during Operation Global Shield 79, the largest, most extensive Strategic Air Command exercise since the 1960s. *National Archives*

Emblazoned on the rudders of SR-71A, USAF serial number 61-7976, is the emblem of the 9th Strategic Reconnaissance Wing. The aircraft is shown during a flight out of Beale Air Force Base during Operation Global Shield 79 in July 1979. *National Archives*

This view of SR-71A, tail number 17974, shows the minimalistic fuselage to good advantage. The thin wings and minimal fuselage of the Blackbird limited the fuel capacity. Combined with the norm of cruising with continuous afterburner meant that frequent aerial refueling was necessary. *National Archives*

An SR-71A is observed from the lower-right quarter during a flight in 1979. "USAF" was painted in white under the left wing, while a national insignia edged in white was marked on the underside of the right wing. *National Archives*

This photo is a companion piece to the preceding one, observing an SR-71A in flight from the lower-left quarter. Faintly visible on the underside of the fuselage between the leading edges of the wings is a red dot: this was a beacon light. *National Archives*

SR-71A, serial number 61-7976, displays its left side during a flight in July 1979. The emblem of the 9th Strategic Reconnaissance Wing is visible on the rudder, below the tail number. The last three digits of that number, 976, are painted in white on the engine nacelle. *National Archives*

During an exercise that was part of Operation Global Shield 79 in July 1979, SR-71A, serial number 61-7976, touches down for a landing at Beale Air Force Base, California. For the SR-71, the normal approach speed was 175 knots and landing speed was 155 knots. *National Archives*

An SR-71A taxis after landing at Beale Air Force Base, having just completed a mission under Operation Global Shield 79. From this angle, the SR-71A looked every inch the high-tech, space-age military aircraft, with its graceful, aerodynamically smart contours. *National Archives*

Lockheed SR-71, USAF serial number 61-7971, is on public display at Beale Air Force Base in 1982. Faintly visible is a red cover on both of the engine air intakes, snugly fitting around the spikes, also known as the movable center bodies.

Pilots of the 9th Strategic Reconnaissance Wing confer during breakfast at Beale Air Force Base. The two officers to the right are wearing "SR-71/HABU" shoulder patches. The one to the left has a different SR-71 patch with a "3+" reference to Mach 3 and over.

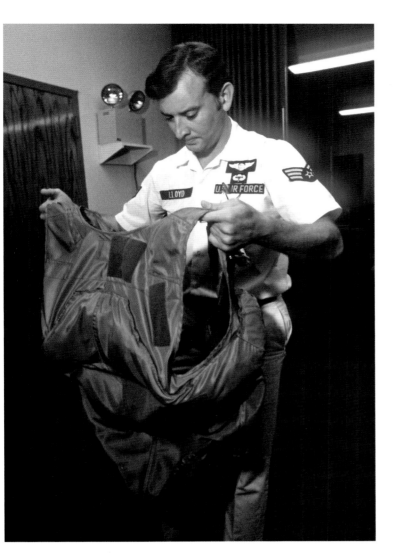

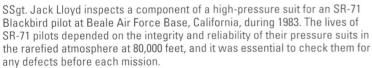

SSgt. Jack Lloyd inspects a component of a high-pressure suit for an SR-71 Blackbird pilot at Beale Air Force Base, California, during 1983. The lives of SR-71 pilots depended on the integrity and reliability of their pressure suits in the rarefied atmosphere at 80,000 feet, and it was essential to check them for any defects before each mission.

High-pressure suits for SR-71 pilots assigned to the 9th Strategic Reconnaissance Wing at Beale Air Force Base hang in a storage. Each suit has an individualized, embroidered shoulder patch containing a United States flag and the name and rank of the wearer. The gloves are attached to the sleeves of the suits by means of dark-colored rings.

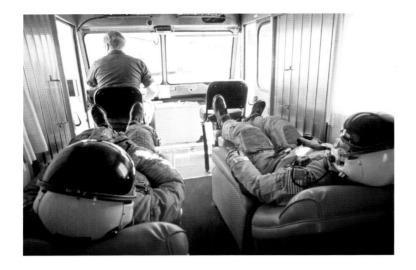

Pilots of the 9th Strategic Reconnaissance Wing are being transported in a specially fitted van to the "barn" or hangar where their SR-71 awaits. They are fully suited and by this point are breathing pure oxygen to purge nitrogen from their bodies prior to high-altitude flight.

Ground crewmen assist pilots of the 9th Strategic Reconnaissance Wing in boarding an SR-71 Blackbird in a hangar at Beale Air Force Base, California, in 1983. Once in the plane, the crew went over their checklists and continued to breathe pure oxygen.

The crew of an SR-71A of the 9th Strategic Reconnaissance Wing sit in the cockpit inside a hangar at Beale Air Force Base in 1983. Visible on the bottom edge of the canopy are four locking latches; between the side windows on the roof of the canopy is padding.

SSgt. David L. Hansen directs the pilot of an SR-71 Blackbird out of its hangar prior to a mission. Because of the limited visibility of the pilot when the canopy was closed, he relied strictly on these hand signals to safely maneuver and taxi the plane.

Taxiing out of a hangar, an SR-71 Blackbird of the 9th Strategic Reconnaissance Wing reveals details of some of its features. For example, around the edges of the windows of the windscreen and the canopy is a thin, red material.

SR-71A, USAF serial number 61-7979, of the 9th Strategic Reconnaissance Wing is readied for takeoff at Beale Air Force Base in 1983. On the rudder below the tail number is the emblem of the 9th Strategic Reconnaissance Wing.

The same SR-71A shown in the preceding photo, serial number 61-7979, takes off from Beale Air Force Base in 1983. Since March 1990, this Blackbird has been on display at the USAF History and Traditions Museum at Lackland Air Force Base, San Antonio, Texas.

An SR-71A Blackbird of the 9th Strategic Reconnaissance Wing is approaching a KC-10 Extender tanker for in-flight refueling during a testing mission out of Beale Air Force Base in 1983. The view is from the refueling-boom operator's station.

In this view from a KC-10 Extender's boom operator's station, the refueling boom has just been connected to the refueling receptacle atop the fuselage of an SR-71A Blackbird of the 9th Strategic Reconnaissance Wing.

Having just landed, following a refueling-test mission in conjunction with a KC-10 Extender tanker, an SR-71A taxis along the flight line at Beale Air Force Base. Atop the rear part of the fuselage are the open doors of the drag-chute compartment.

An SR-71A assigned to the 9th Strategic Reconnaissance Wing taxis along a flight line in August 1983. On top of the rear part of the fuselage, the open doors of the drag parachute, for slowing down the aircraft upon landing, are open. *Department of Defense*

Airmen prepare to assist the pilot of an SR-71A of the 9th Strategic Reconnaissance Wing to exit from the cockpit. The plane was undergoing test refuelings from a KC-10 Extender tanker. *Department of Defense*

An SR-71A assigned to Detachment (Det) 4, 9th Strategic Reconnaissance Wing, Third Air Force, readies for takeoff from RAF Mildenhall, England, in September 1983. A red beacon light aft of the nose landing gear is illuminated. *Department of Defense*

The full power of the afterburners gives the necessary boost for an SR-71A of Det 4, 9th Strategic Reconnaissance Wing, to lift off from a fog-encased runway at RAF Mildenhall, September 1983. The landing gear is in the process being retracted. *Department of Defense*

Lockheed SR-71A, serial number 61-7974, of the 9th Strategic Reconnaissance Wing approaches the refueling boom of a KC-135 Stratotanker in September 1983. This SR-71 was lost on April 21, 1989, following an engine explosion during takeoff from Kadena Air Base, Okinawa. *Department of Defense*

A low sun glints off the underside of an SR-71A Blackbird with landing gear extended in September 1983. It may be seen that the left rudder is turned hard to the left. The tail number, 17974 (serial number 61-7974), is very faintly visible on the rudder. *Department of Defense*

A shadowy SR-71A buzzes the flight line at Beale Air Force Base in honor of Brig. Gen. Jesse S. Hocker, former commander of the 14th Air Division, during his retirement ceremony in 1984. The general was associated with bombardment wings throughout his career. *Department of Defense*

Capt. William D. Stanford helps the actor Craig T. Nelson strap into the pilot's seat of an SR-71A in September 1984. A production crew for the TV series *Call to Glory* was filming Nelson, who portrayed Col. Sarnac in the series, for footage to re-create the early SR-71 flights. *Department of Defense*

Physiological Support Division technicians at Beale Air Force Base fit Gen. Larry D. Welch into a pressure suit prior to his first flight in a Lockheed SR-71 Blackbird. At the time, in September 1987, Gen. Welch was commander in chief of Strategic Air Command. The technician to the right is securing the helmet to the pressure suit. *Department of Defense*

The air shimmers from the heat issuing from the twin jet exhausts of a Lockheed SR-71A as it taxis prior to takeoff at an unidentified base in September 1985. The chines of the fuselage and the engine nacelle were made of composite materials with high heat resistance. *Department of Defense*

Ground crewmen perform maintenance on an SR-71 at MacDill Air Force Base, Florida, in September 1987. One preflight maintenance challenge was the necessity of using a special cart to preheat the Blackbird's hydraulic system to in-flight temperatures. *Department of Defense*

Flight crews and security policemen assemble near an SR-71A participating in Air Fete '88, a NATO aircraft display hosted by the 513th Airborne Command and Control Wing at RAF Mildenhall in May 1988. French Alpha Jets are in the background. *Department of Defense*

Spectators congregate around an SR-71A on display at RAF Mildenhall during Air Fete '88 in May 1988. A fence around the perimeter of the Blackbird display kept the crowd at a respectful distance, preventing them from seeing too many of the details of this spy plane. *Department of Defense*

A vigilant Air Force security policeman stands guard over an SR-71A parked at MacDill Air Force Base in September 1987. Security policemen guarded the SR-71s wherever they were based. For example, 9th Security Police Squadron fulfilled this task at Beale Air Force Base. *Department of Defense*

A Lockheed SR-71 Blackbird is parked in a hangar at an undisclosed air base in June 1989. A red "remove before flight" tag is hanging from the pitot tube on the nose. Black-colored covers are installed on all the wheels of the landing gear. *Department of Defense*

A Lockheed-employed ground crewman with that company's logo on the back of his shirt is signaling the pilot of an SR-71 preparatory to takeoff, in June 1989. Throughout the SR-71's history, Lockheed provided ongoing technical support in the factory and in the field. *Department of Defense*

In a photograph related to the preceding one, an SR-71 about to take off from an undisclosed air base is viewed close-up and head-on during September 1989. At this point, the SR-71s were only a few months away from retirement. *Department of Defense*

An SR-71A approaches a KC-135Q Stratotanker for refueling. A total of thirty-five Stratotankers were converted to KC-135Qs for refueling SR-71s either in the air or, when required, on the ground. *Department of Defense*

An SR-71A Blackbird is viewed from the boom operator's station aboard a KC-135Q Stratotanker. The door of the refueling receptacle on the fuselage deck to the rear of the cockpit is open. The tail number is in red but is indecipherable. The layout of the red lines delineating the permissible areas for walking on the wings is readily visible. *Department of Defense*

Another view from the boom operator's station in a tanker aircraft shows an SR-71A at close range, here again with the door of the refueling receptacle open and ready to make a connection with the refueling boom. Red stencils are visible on the fuselage around the cockpit. Streaking from spilled jet fuel is apparent on the fuselage deck to the rear of the refueling receptacle. *Department of Defense*

The special paint on SR-71s, as seen here in September 1989, had black pigmentation containing tiny iron balls, which dissipated electromagnetically generated energy and friction-generated heat and reduced the plane's radar signature. *Department of Defense*

An SR-71A cruises high over the desert in September 1989. The black, iron-ball paint lowered the Blackbird's radar signature by converting radar waves into heat, which then was dissipated into the atmosphere. The F-117 Nighthawk used the same type of paint. *Department of Defense*

A ground crewman and an SR-71A are silhouetted at a desert air base in 1990. By then the twenty-one-year operational career of the Blackbird was about to end, the US Air Force having decided to decommission its SR-71 fleet that year. *Department of Defense*

Ben Rich (1925–95), the propulsion-systems chief engineer for the SR-71 program and, from 1975, Kelly Johnson's successor as director of Lockheed's Skunk Works, poses for his photograph in front of an SR-71A in 1990. *Stan Piet collection*

An SR-71A serving with the 9th Strategic Reconnaissance Wing maneuvers above a snowy, mountainous landscape during a flight out of Beale Air Force Base, California, in about 1990. The insignia of the 9th Strategic Reconnaissance Wing is visible on the left rudder. Serving this wing at Beale were the 349th and 350th Air Refueling Squadrons. *Department of Defense*

In 1990 an SR-71A is refueled in flight. In the early years of the Blackbird, often three tankers would be dispatched to refuel an SR-71, in order to allow for enough fuel for the plane as well as to have an extra tanker near by in case of refueling problems. Later, the Air Force limited SR-71 refueling missions to one tanker. *Department of Defense*

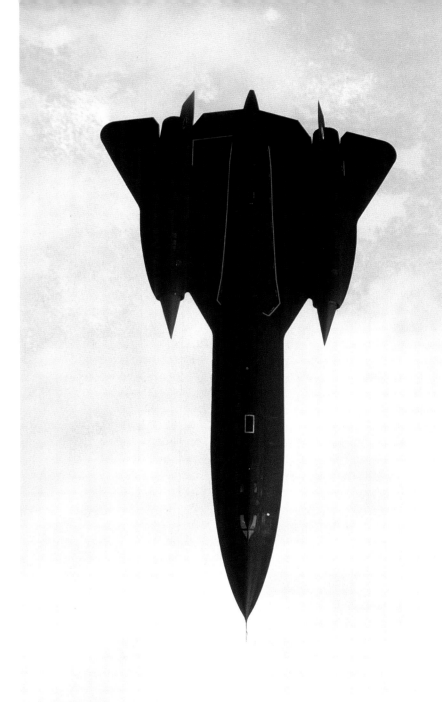

An SR-71 of the 9th Strategic Reconnaissance Wing flies above high clouds during a refueling rendezvous with a tanker in about 1990. A light-red or orange border may be seen around the port of the refueling receptacle on the fuselage, aft of the cockpits. Tankers were required to be on station thirty minutes before the arrival of the SR-71, to monitor the weather and establish their refueling orbits. *Department of Defense*

A tractor tows an SR-71A from the runway at Mountain Home Air Force Base in Idaho following an emergency landing around early 1990. The aircraft had developed a hydraulic leak during a test flight out of Palmdale, California, and had been forced to land. *Department of Defense*

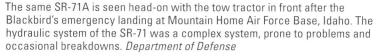

The same SR-71A is seen head-on with the tow tractor in front after the Blackbird's emergency landing at Mountain Home Air Force Base, Idaho. The hydraulic system of the SR-71 was a complex system, prone to problems and occasional breakdowns. *Department of Defense*

An even closer view shows the same Blackbird from the front at Mountain Home in about 1990. The pilot's canopy had a single actuator: this is the light-colored vertical cylinder visible in the rear of the cockpit, on the pilot's left-hand side. *Department of Defense*

What was supposed to be the final USAF operational flight of an SR-71A was on January 26, 1990. The aircrew on that mission, Lt. Col. Thomas E. Bergam, *third from left*, and Lt. Col. William R. Dyckman, *fourth from left*, pose after the flight with officials from Lockheed and the Air Force. *Department of Defense*

The aircrew of SR-71A, serial number 61-7960, Lt. Col. William R. Dyckman, *left*, and Lt. Col. Thomas E. Bergam, disembark from the plane upon completion of the last operational flight of a Blackbird, at Beale Air Force Base, California, on January 26, 1990. *Department of Defense*

SR-71A, serial number 61-7975, of the 9th Strategic Reconnaissance Wing is seen at the time of its deactivation ceremony in late February 1990. The aircrew, Maj. Terry B. Pappas and Maj. John D. Manzi, would fly the aircraft to March Field, California, for permanent display. *Department of Defense*

The same SR-71A shown in the preceding photo is viewed head-on as it taxis along a flight line prior to its deactivation ceremony in February 1990. Mounted on the nose landing-gear strut are a 1,000-watt landing light and a 450-watt taxi light. Jutting from the nose is the combination pitot tube and alpha-beta probe, with two separate tips. *Department of Defense*

The focus is on the right engine nacelle and inlet spike of SR-71A, USAF serial number 61-7975, as it arrives for its deactivation ceremony in February 1990. The inlet spikes were automatically locked in the forward position, as seen here, during operations on the ground as well as during flights below an altitude of 30,000 feet. *Department of Defense*

Spectators have assembled to witness the deactivation ceremony of SR-71A, USAF serial number 61-7975, of the 9th Strategic Reconnaissance Wing in February 1990. In the background is an assortment of USAF aircraft, including a U-2 spy plane to the left. *Department of Defense*

Maj. Terry B. Pappas, pilot, and Maj. John D. Manzi, reconnaissance systems officer, prepare to exit the cockpits of SR-71, serial number 61-7975, at the time of the plane's deactivation ceremony. Both crewmen are wearing white helmets and tan pressure suits with US flag shoulder patches. *Department of Defense*

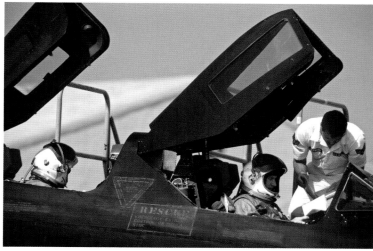

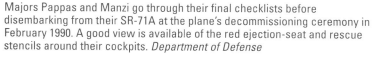

Majors Pappas and Manzi go through their final checklists before disembarking from their SR-71A at the plane's decommissioning ceremony in February 1990. A good view is available of the red ejection-seat and rescue stencils around their cockpits. *Department of Defense*

Maj. Terry B. Pappas (*left*) and his RSO, Maj. John D. Manzi, stand next to their SR-71A after delivering the plane for its deactivation ceremony. On the sleeves of their pressure suits are patches with printed emergency-egress checklists. *Department of Defense*

SR-71A, serial number 61-7972, rests in a hangar at Lockheed Corporation headquarters before its March 6, 1990, coast-to-coast flight. The plane would set new performance records during the flight to its new home at the National Air and Space Museum in Washington, DC. *Department of Defense*

Lieutenant Col. Yeilding adjusts his inner gloves prior to his March 6, 1990, coast-to-coast flight. Outer, pressurized gloves would then be attached to the ring-shaped locks on the sleeves of the David Clark pressure suit. The helmet had a fiberglass outer shell and both a clear visor and a tinted visor, which are raised in this photo. *Department of Defense*

Lt. Col. Raymond E. Yeilding, pilot, has suited up in preparation for his record-breaking coast-to-coast flight in SR-71A, serial number 61-7972, on March 6, 1990. He flew the route from Los Angeles to Washington, DC, in sixty-eight minutes. In the back seat was Lt. Col. Joseph T. Vida, reconnaissance systems officer. Both crewmen were assigned to Det 6, 2762nd Logistics Squadron. *Department of Defense*

Blackbird Records

Date	Aircraft	Crew	Record
1 May 1965	YF-12A 60-6934	Col. Robert L. Stephens & Lt. Col. David Andre	Absolute altitude record, 80,257.86 feet
1 May 1965	YF-12A 60-6936	Col. Robert L. Stephens & Lt. Col. David Andre	Absolute speed record, 2,070.1 mph
26 April 1971	SR-71A 61-7968	Thomas Estes & Dewain Vick	Mackay and Harmon Trophies for over 15,000 miles in 10 hours, 30 minutes
1 Sept 1974	SR-71A 61-7972	James Sullivan & Noel Widdfield	New York to London, 1 hour, 54 minutes, 56.4 seconds (avg. 1,807 mph)
13 Sept 1974	SR-71A 61-7972	Harold Adams & William Machorek	London to Los Angeles, 3,227 minutes, 38 seconds (avg. 1,435.59 mph)
28 July 1976	SR-71A 61-7962	Robert Helt & Larry Elliott	Absolute altitude record, 85,069 feet
28 July 1976	SR-71A 61-7958	Eldon Joersz & George Morgan	Absolute speed record, 2,193,2 mph
6 March 1990	SR-71A 61-7972	Raymond Yeilding & Joseph Vida	LA to Washington, DC, 2,299.7 miles, 64 minutes, 20 seconds (avg. 2144.8 mph)
6 March 1990	SR-71A 61-7972	Raymond Yeilding & Joseph Vida	West Coast to East Coast, 2,404 miles, 67 minutes, 54 seconds (avg. 2,124.5 mph)
6 March 1990	SR-71A 61-7972	Raymond Yeilding & Joseph Vida	Kansas City, MO, to Washington DC, 942 miles, 25 minutes, 59 seconds (2,176 mph)
6 March 1990	SR-71A 61-7972	Raymond Yeilding & Joseph Vida	St. Louis to Cincinnati, 311.4 miles, 8 minutes, 32 seconds (2,189.9 mph)

Eleven SR-71 Blackbirds are arrayed on a hardstand at Beale Air Force Base, California. During a large part of the Cold War, these Blackbirds and others served the United States well, gathering intelligence on the nation's adversaries and serving as test vehicles for advances in aeronautical design and high-speed aviation. *Stan Piet collection*

Displayed at the Stephen F. Udvar-Hazy Center, National Air and Space Museum (NASM) Annex, Chantilly, Virginia, is this SR-71 Blackbird, serial number 61-7972. This aircraft was rolled out on December 12, 1966, and it amassed 2,801 flying hours before its retirement. In 1985 this Blackbird became a Lockheed Skunk Works test aircraft at Palmdale, California. During its delivery flight from Palmdale to the NASM on March 6, 1990, the plane set several records. *David Doyle*

The nose landing gear is observed from the left front. The tires for the SR-71s were by B. F. Goodrich and were filled with nitrogen, to reduce the chances of fire in the event a tire exploded. A 1,000-watt landing light and a 450-watt taxi light are mounted on the oleo strut. *David Doyle*

The nose landing gear and the left landing-gear-bay door are viewed from the right side. The gear swiveled to the front when being retracted. The doors were mechanically linked to the nose-gear strut in order to operate the doors. *David Doyle*

In a frontal view of SR-71, serial number 61-7972, protruding from the nose is the pitot tube, with the alpha/beta probe jutting from its side. The alpha/beta probe was for measuring incidence and yaw. A jack is supporting the bottom of the nose landing gear, to keep the weight off the tires. *David Doyle*

The nose landing gear is seen from the left side. The nose gear was steerable to 45 degrees to the left or right of center. To the rear of the oleo strut is the antitorque "scissors" link. *David Doyle*

The forward parts of the nose landing-gear-bay doors are seen from the front left. Ventilation grilles are on the forward ends of the doors, as well as on the rear ends. *David Doyle*

As seen in a view of the left main landing gear from the front-left quarter, each gear had three wheels and tires. The thirty-two-ply tires, by B. F. Goodrich, were of rubber infused with powdered aluminum to give the tires a higher flash point, to withstand the friction-induced high temperatures of high-speed landings. All tires were filled with nitrogen to 400 psi. *David Doyle*

The left main landing gear is viewed from the rear. Jacks to each side of the center tire are supporting the gear. To the left of the oleo strut is the outer landing-gear-bay door, which is mechanically linked to the strut. Running to the right from the strut is the landing-gear actuator. *David Doyle*

Two inboard doors for the main landing-gear bays are located along the centerline of the fuselage. These doors also served to lock the main gear in the retracted position. *David Doyle*

The pilot's and reconnaissance systems officer's canopies are observed from the right side. Below each canopy is a red stencil with a warning that a seat with an explosive charge is inside. Between the canopies are, *top*, an ejection-seat warning sign, and, *bottom*, a "RESCUE" warning that the emergency-entrance control is on the other side of the fuselage. *David Doyle*

On the outer side of the left rudder are, *from top to bottom*, the crest of the Air Force Logistics Command, tail number 17972, both of which are in red, and the symbol of the Skunk Works. *David Doyle*

The right outer-wing panel, rudder, engine exhaust nozzle, and engine nacelle are featured in this elevated view of the NASM's SR-71. *David Doyle*

The fuselage, right rudder, engine nacelle, engine exhaust nozzle, and outer wing panel are viewed from above. Some details of the inner sides of the "turkey feathers" are visible in the exhaust nozzle. *David Doyle*

The fuselage and the engine nacelles are viewed from above, looking forward. The corrugated skin on the inner wing panels assisted with skin expansion at high temperatures. *David Doyle*

The left rudder, engine nacelle, and wing are observed from above. Faintly visible on the nacelle above the front end of the red walkway stripe on the wing are blow-in doors for supplying tertiary air to the ejector nozzle. *David Doyle*

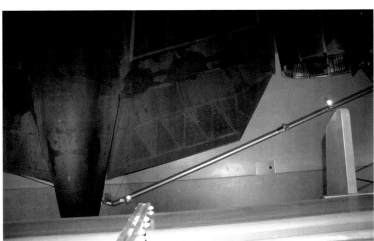

From left to right, as viewed from above, are part of the tail cone of the SR-71, the right inboard elevon, and the right engine exhaust nozzle. *David Doyle*

The left outer wing panel, exhaust nozzle, and rudder are seen from above. Faintly visible along the leading and trailing edges of the elevon are the triangular shapes of the high-temperature plastic composite panels, designed to tolerate the extremely high temperatures that developed on the surfaces at high altitudes and high speeds. *David Doyle*

The top of the pilot's seat, the interiors of the canopies, and details in the front cockpit to the right rear of the pilot's seat are visible in this SR-71A. The headrest was of a semigloss bright-red color. A thin red border was around the windscreen glass. *Department of Defense*

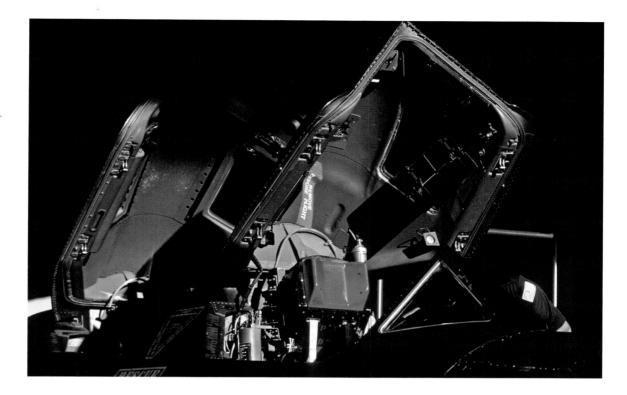

To the left on the instrument panel inside the pilot's cockpit of an SR-71 are air-conditioning controls, while to the right is the fuel and electrical control panel. In between are flight and navigational instruments and displays. *Department of Defense*

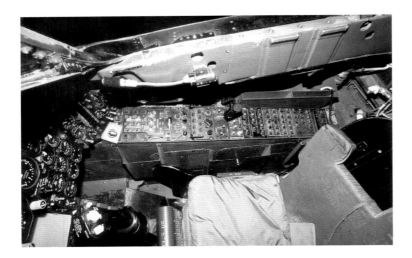

The right console of the SR-71 front cockpit contained, *front to rear*, control panels for the automatic flight-control system, the TACAN system, the interphone, cabin pressure, and VHF radio. The pilot's seat is to the lower right. *Department of Defense*

On the left console of the front cockpit were, *to the front*, the roll-trim rudder sync panel, the throttle quadrant, and the control panel for the map display. Farther back were the oxygen control panel, the UHF-1 radio control panel, and other controls. *Department of Defense*

In this photograph of the rear cockpit of an SR-71, at the center of the instrument panel is, *top*, the electro-optical view-sight display, below which is the RSO's map projector. Various gauges and controls are to the sides. The front ends of the consoles are at the bottom. *Department of Defense*

Lockheed SR-71, serial number 61-7973, is on static display at the Blackbird Airpark, Palmdale, California. This Blackbird's first flight was on February 8, 1967, and it logged 1,729.9 hours of flight during its career. *David Dwight Jackson*

Starting in 1990. NASA operated Lockheed SR-712A, serial number 61-7980, from the NASA Dryden Flight Research Center, at Edwards Air Force Base, California. NASA assigned the aircraft number 844 while employing it in high-altitude and high-speed tests and experiments. The plane is on outdoor display at NASA Armstrong Flight Research Center, Edwards Air Force Base, California. *David Dwight Jackson*

The SR-71B, of which only two were completed, was a two-seat trainer version of the Blackbird. It was distinguished by the prominent, bulged rear canopy. Construction of this SR-71B, serial number 61-7956, commenced on June 18, 1964, and the plane was rolled out on May 20, 1965. Its first flight was on November 18, 1965. The aircraft is seen here later that year, just before its delivery to Beale Air Force Base, California. *National Archives*

SR-71B, serial number 61-7956, is viewed from the right side. The raised rear cockpit for the instructor pilot (IP) is apparent; it was equipped with a windscreen for the IP's forward visibility. This aircraft now is on display at the Kalamazoo Aviation History Museum in Michigan. *National Archives*

The only SR-71C, serial number 61-7981 was created by mating the rear fuselage of the first YF-12A, serial number 60-6934, with the forward fuselage of an SR-71A static test article. The impetus for this was a shortage of SR-71B trainers following the loss of 61-7957 in January 1968. First flown on March 14, 1969, the SR-71C was dubbed "the bastard" because of its unorthodox creation as well as its stability and maintenance problems; the aircraft last flew on April 11, 1976. *Brian C. Rogers*

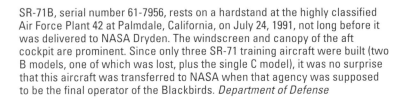

SR-71B, serial number 61-7956, rests on a hardstand at the highly classified Air Force Plant 42 at Palmdale, California, on July 24, 1991, not long before it was delivered to NASA Dryden. The windscreen and canopy of the aft cockpit are prominent. Since only three SR-71 training aircraft were built (two B models, one of which was lost, plus the single C model), it was no surprise that this aircraft was transferred to NASA when that agency was supposed to be the final operator of the Blackbirds. *Department of Defense*

The flight crew of an SR-71B pose for their portrait to the front of their Blackbird at MacDill Air Force Base, Florida, in September 1987. Their ranks (*captain to the left, major to the right*) and names (*illegible*) are on patches above the US flag shoulder patches. *Department of Defense*

The following series of images show SR-71B, serial number 61-7956, at the time of its 1,000th sortie, on January 15, 1982. For the occasion, special white markings were applied to the aircraft, including the words "1000th SORTIE" on the rudders and "1000th FLT." on the underside of the fuselage. *Department of Defense*

High-visibility white markings on the underside of the left side of the fuselage commemorate the 1,000th flight of SR-71B, serial number 61-7956. Unlike the SR-71As, the SR-71Bs had a ventral fin under each engine nacelle for better directional stability. *Department of Defense*

SR-71B, serial number 61-7956, soars high over a mountain range during its 1,000th training sortie. The aircrew for this flight consisted of Lt. Col. David M. Peters and Maj. Gerald T. Glasser of the 1st Strategic Reconnaissance Squadron. The two SR-71Bs were not equipped with any reconnaissance or intelligence-gathering sensors. *Department of Defense*

As SR-71B, serial number 61-7956, banks over a snowy mountain range, its two ventral fins become clearly visible. The 1,000th sortie markings are not present on the aircraft here. Since 2003, this Blackbird has been on exhibition at the Kalamazoo Aviation History Museum, in Kalamazoo, Michigan. *Department of Defense*

Ground crewmen are preparing for the disembarkation of Lt. Col. David M. Peters and Maj. Gerald T. Glasser following the 1,000th sortie of SR-71B, serial number 61-7956, on January 15, 1982. Red chocks have been snugged up to the main landing-gear tires. *Department of Defense*

In this time-exposure photograph taken shortly after sundown, red lights from moving aircraft streak across the background behind an SR-71B Blackbird on a hardstand. Red inlet covers are visible on the fronts of the engine nacelles. *Department of Defense*

CHAPTER 5
NASA Grants a Brief Reprieve

As previously seen, NASA was provided YF-12s, and an SR-71A masquerading as a YF-12C, as far back as 1969. In NASA hands, these early experiments with the aircraft yielded valuable research data—enough to fill 125 technical reports—on such subjects as aerodynamics, propulsion, controls, structures, subsystems, and other areas such as the physics of the upper atmosphere, noise tests, and measurements. Despite this, the early YF-12-centered test program was discontinued in 1979.

When word reached NASA that the Air Force was looking to discontinue the SR-71 program in 1989–90, the agency immediately expressed a desire to obtain some of the surplus (one can hardly use the word "obsolete" to describe an aircraft the remains the fastest, highest-flying, air-breathing, manned aircraft in the world!) Blackbirds and support equipment.

On February 12, 1990, NASA's Dryden Research Center received SR-71A 61-7980 / NASA 844. SR-71A (61-7971 / NASA 832) arrived at Dryden on March 19, 1990. Also, NASA agreed to fund the completion of the overhaul, begun by the Air Force, of SR-71B 61-7956 (NASA 831), which arrived at Dryden on July 25, 1991, and served as a research platform as well as for crew training and proficiency until October 1997. To further aid pilot training, NASA took possession of the recently refurbished Singer-Link simulator. The remaining SR-71 spare parts were also transferred to NASA, which stored them at the nearby Marine Corps Logistics Base, Barstow, California.

In 1995, when the Air Force SR-71 program was reactivated, the 832 was returned to Air Force inventory as the first aircraft reactivated.

NASA's final flight of the Blackbird—indeed the final flight of *any* Blackbird—was made by 844 (61-7980) on October 9, 1999, reaching Mach 3.21 and 80,100 feet at an air show at Edwards Air Force Base.

Although the Air Force had studied the potential for reactivating the SR-71 in 2001, following the September 11 attacks, determining the cost for reactivation and first-year operation would be $45 million, with the second-year operation costs projected at $40 million; this was not to be. In October 2007, the spare-parts stockpile at Barstow was destroyed by an Air Force disposal team, forever ending the chance of returning an SR-71 to the air.

The Air Force transferred SR-71A, serial number 61-7980, to NASA in 1990 for high-speed flight research. It was based at NASA Dryden Flight Research Center, California, and bore NASA number 844. In 2002, this plane was placed on display at the Dryden Flight Research Center. *Department of Defense*

SR-71A, serial number 61-7980, has just arrived for duty at NASA Dryden Flight Research Center at Edwards Air Force Base, California, in March 1990. There, the plane would be redubbed with NASA number 844 and employed in NASA's high-speed aviation research. *Department of Defense*

US Air Force markings are still present on SR-71A, serial number 61-7980, in this NASA photo of the plane taking off during 1990. This Blackbird survives and currently is on static display inside the main gate at the NASA Dryden facility. *Department of Defense*

The red drag chute has deployed to slow down SR-71A, serial number 61-7980, during a landing in 1990. The drag chute had a diameter of 40 feet, and, in addition to slowing the aircraft, it also served to reduce tire wear and brake deterioration. *Department of Defense*

NASA SR-71A number 844 formerly USAF serial number 61-7980, flies over a mountain range during 1992. On the rudder is the NASA logo in red over a white band, with dark-colored edging on the top and bottom, with aircraft number 844 below the logo. *Department of Defense*

NASA SR-71A number 844 flies during an experiment dealing with ultraviolet light in 1994. The engines are producing shock diamonds, also called Mach diamonds, standing-wave patterns influenced by variations in atmospheric pressure.

NASA SR-71A number 844 is parked on a ramp at the Dryden Flight Research Center at Edwards Air Force Base in April 1994. With this plane's ability to produce heat-soak temperatures of over 600 degrees Fahrenheit, it was well suited for NASA thermal experiments. *Department of Defense*

When NASA began operating the SR-71 on a regular basis as part of its high-speed flight research program, the agency received SR-71B, serial number 61-7956. As it had for the Air Force, the SR-71B served NASA as a pilot trainer. While in NASA service it wore the tail number 831 and flew from the Ames/Dryden Flight Research Center (Edwards Air Force Base). *NASA via Carla Thomas*

NASA SR-71A number 844 is parked at Dryden Flight Research Center in April 1994. One major NASA experiment with its SR-71A was a laser air-data collection system, employing laser light instead of air pressure to produce airspeed and attitude reference data. *Department of Defense*

As seen on February 15, 1996, LASRE (Linear Aerospike SR-71 Experiment) involved mounting a half-span model of the Lockheed Martin X-33 lifting body (the white object partially hiding the flag) on the tail of the NASA SR-71A. *Department of Defense*

Technicians mount the LASRE package on NASA SR-71A number 844 on February 15, 1996. The X-33 model included eight thrust cells of an aerospike engine. The goal of the experiment was to pave the way for a future reusable launch vehicle. *Department of Defense*

The white, triangular object above the rear of the SR-71A is the LASRE package. It rested on the top rear of a long, streamlined base, which bore the logos of Lockheed Martin, Rockwell Aerospace, and Rocketdyne, and NASA and Air Force insignia. *Department of Defense*

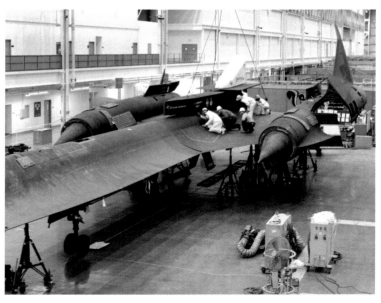

Technicians at the Lockheed Martin Skunk Works, Palmdale, California, are test-fitting the LASRE package, supported by cables from an overhead crane, on the rear of the fuselage of SR-71 number 844 in February 1996. *Department of Defense*

The test-fitting of the LASRE package on the rear of SR-71 number 844 at NASA Dryden in February 1996 is seen from a different perspective. The movable parts of the rudders, removed while the LASRE was being installed, are here visible to the right. *Department of Defense*

The LASRE package has been installed and the rudders remounted on NASA SR-71A number 844 prior to its first test flight on October 31, 1997. The experiment included two initial flights for purposes of safety, and five flights in which experiments were conducted. *Department of Defense*

On October 31, 1997, NASA's SR-71A flies by on its first flight with the experimental package mounted on its rear fuselage. Despite the extraordinary measures undertaken to advance the LASRE program, in March 2001 NASA canceled the Lockheed Martin X-33 program. *Department of Defense*

The LASRE package on the NASA SR-71A is being ground-tested in this view of the rear of the aircraft. On the side of the white-colored portion of the package is written "LASRE" above "LINEAR AEROSPIKE SR-71 EXPERIMENT." *Department of Defense*

The LASRE package is dumping water into the atmosphere in the aftermath of its first in-flight cold-flow test on March 4, 1998. These experimental flights were akin to using the SR-71 as a flying wind tunnel for the LASRE model. *Department of Defense*

Afterburners glowing and landing gear in the process of retracting, the NASA SR-71A (number 844) takes off on a test mission with the LASRE package on March 4, 1998. This was the occasion of the first cold-flow test of the LASRE system. *Department of Defense*

In 1997, NASA's Dryden Flight Research Center staged this gathering of research aircraft. *Left to right*, the outer arc consists of X-31, F-15, SR-71B, F-106B, F-16XL, and X-38. Directly ahead of the SR-71 is the X-36, and to its right the Radio Control Mothership. Although the second-oldest aircraft design represented, the SR-71 is easily the fastest and highest flying of the group, as well as the largest. *NASA*

Shock diamonds issue from the exhausts of NASA's SR-71B number 831 during a
1992 experimental flight. Whether it was strategic aerial-reconnaissance missions
in heavily defended enemy airspace, or more-peaceful experimental flights
exploring the boundaries of high-speed, high-altitude flight, the SR-71 Blackbird
was a reliable, sophisticated aircraft, and one that its crewmen, the "Habus,"
were proud to fly. *Department of Defense*